# Death

## NEED NOT BE

# FATAL

# *Death*
# NEED NOT BE
# FATAL

## MALACHY McCOURT

with

## BRIAN McDONALD

CENTER
STREET

NEW YORK NASHVILLE

Center Street
Hachette Book Group
1290 Avenue of the Americas, New York, NY 10104
centerstreet.com
twitter.com/centerstreet

First Edition: May 2017

Center Street is a division of Hachette Book Group, Inc. The Center Street name and logo are trademarks of Hachette Book Group, Inc.

The publisher is not responsible for websites (or their content) that are not owned by the publisher.

The Hachette Speakers Bureau provides a wide range of authors for speaking events. To find out more, go to www.HachetteSpeakersBureau.com or call (866) 376-6591.

Library of Congress Cataloging-in-Publication Data has been applied for.

ISBN: 9781478917069 (hardcover), 9781478917052 (ebook)

Printed in the United States of America

LSC-C

10  9  8  7  6  5  4  3  2  1

*For Fiona, Mark, Adrianna, Gillian, Reilly, Gus, Cassidy, and Cole. Thank you for the energy the love the laughter the light and joy you bring into our lives as the grandest of grandchildren.*

# Contents

# Death

## NEED NOT BE

# FATAL

# Notes from the Departure Lounge

Come into my mind, come on into my mind, which is leaping about trying to have a bit of merriment at the prospect of the ending of my life. Here's the situation, though it's hard to conceive. Like yourself, I am a member of a species that has a 100 percent mortality rate. Try as I might to be an exception, I will someday in the not-too-distant future expire, depart, ascend, vanish, or exit from this earth.

———

The advent of death is a simple procedure, as is the advent of life. It's our time on the stage coming to its final curtain call. In our so-called civilized world, a trained medical person detaches a baby from its mother's body and gives the little creature a whack on the arse, which causes the very first inhalation of air that marks the beginning of life. At the end of life, and hopefully many inhalations later, the body gives one last exhalation, which sends a breath into the atmosphere, and when it attempts to return to the lung it finds the doorway locked, blocked, closed forever, thus rendering that last breath homeless, left only to disintegrate and join the prevailing atmosphere.

This happens to about 6,500 humans every hour of every day in our world, two per second, as Death is an equal-opportunity laddie and quite a random fellow; he doesn't mind whether you are a man, a child, or a woman if he needs to fill his daily quota. Some people, if old and sickly, put out the welcome mat for him, whilst others, who are young and healthy, leave behind friends and relatives aghast and enraged that fate has dispatched their loved ones too soon by putting them on the doomed plane, allowing them to inject too much heroin, or being in the back seat while a friend texted behind the wheel.

Though I haven't put the welcome mat out, I do now resemble a slow-moving mobile human tenement, with various body parts and organs disintegrating, falling down, and otherwise bidding me a slow farewell, though the mind appears intact, with leakage fairly well under control.

As I am in my eighties, though, and there are far fewer tomorrows ahead and more yesteryears behind, I am essentially hanging out in the departure lounge, waiting for the call to board the last transport to somewhere. All things considered, it isn't a bad vantage from which to observe the rest of my life. Nice in here. There's roasted peanuts, sparkly water, and neatly uniformed lads and lasses with white, white teeth. The windows stretch from floor to ceiling, offering an unobstructed view of the takeoffs. Last travelers, and friends and relatives seeing them off, surround me.

Unlike the ones in Kennedy Airport or O'Hare or Shannon,

the lounge in which I sit, however, offers no travel brochures. You don't know for sure whether you're headed to Cancún or the Swiss Alps, or maybe even Disney World, which is sort of like purgatory. Nothing is set in stone.

The various religions seem to agree on the existence of heaven and hell. In one version, that of the religion of my youth, heaven is a very busy place inhabited by about 2.5 billion men, women, and children who have been told that their reward for years of piety and chastity is the privilege of sitting at the right hand of God and gazing at his right earlobe for all eternity, which is fine if you're a lobe lover.

Down below, on the other hand, is a place of perpetual fire with a long line of folk who have been sent there for unreported offenses against the God Guy. It's a very active environment, where the original staff is forever employed in sticking red-hot pokers and pitchforks into the orifices of the guests. James Joyce said the lake of fire there is boundless, shoreless, and bottomless. A place where "the blood seethes and boils in the veins, the brains are boiling in the skull, the bowels a red-hot mass of burning pulp, the tender eyes flaming like molten balls."

Imagine, the famed Irish writer said, "some foul and putrid corpse that has lain rotting and decomposing in the grave, a jelly-like mass of liquid corruption. Imagine such a corpse a prey to flames, devoured by the fire of burning brimstone and giving off dense choking fumes of nauseous loathsome decomposition. And then imagine this sickening stench, multiplied a millionfold and a millionfold again from the millions upon millions of fetid carcasses massed together in the reeking darkness, a huge and rotting human fungus. Imagine all this, and you will have some idea of the horror of the stench of hell."

I've had mornings like that.

Saint Augustine tells us that one of the perks of heaven is that God gives you a front-row seat to a television monitor of sorts with a live (or dead) feed right from hell, so you can see the suffering there in real time! Fox broadcasts it, I think.

The whole business of the afterlife is of great interest to me, and this book is not my first attempt at mining this rich material. I once told an editor from a major publisher that I was looking to get an advance for a book about death I was going to write after I died.

"But that's never been done," she replied.

"Exactly!" I said.

Though I'm still waiting for the check, I own the belief that we don't, nor will we ever, know what's next, and that thought can either frighten or intrigue you.

I'll take the intrigue, thank you.

From my seat here in the departure lounge, I will explore the role death has played and continues to play in my life and in the world I've inhabited for the past eighty-five years. From the poverty-stricken Limerick of my childhood, to Angela's famous ashes, to the deaths of a baby sister and all my brothers—and my own impending demise—the Grim Reaper has been a constant companion and reminder of what is important, and, just as important, what's not. I am somewhat of an elderly orphan.

As the last of the Limerick generation of McCourts (the youngest brother, Alphie, died suddenly in July of 2016) I've also found myself in the position of being the final singer of the McCourt song, and self-charged with the responsibility of filling whatever gaps there are and correcting the record, as it were. I'll try to keep the lies to a minimum, but I never let the truth get in the way of a good story, and a lie is just a dream that might come true.

————

Finally, I intend in the pages ahead to explore the vast expanse of belief in both the religious and spiritual arenas. They are different, you know. I belong to a disorganization whose members strive, one day at a time, to stay clean, sober, and helpful to each other and the human race at large. One of the more favored sayings in this very nonselect club is that religious people are afraid of going to hell, while spiritual people have already been there. The Limerick of my youth qualifies me as spiritual.

I've come a long way in my beliefs. I started life as a captive of the One Holy Roman Catholic Apostolic Church, and I am coming to the end of it without organized religion or mystical thinking. I'm an atheist, thank God, with no fear of hell and no hope of heaven.

People tell me all the time, "Well, you don't believe in anything, then!" How wrong they are. I am an atheist six days a week and a pagan on Sunday. I believe in sunrises and flowers and babbling brooks and waterfalls and moonlight and stars and rainstorms. I've often been told, as I'm sure you have too, that if I want to see God all I have to do is look into the face of a child. This I agree with; I have been blessed with grandchildren whose laughter is the sweetest music to my ears.

I also believe that you can see God in the elderly, and newly married couples, and even teenagers with plugs in their earlobes and spikes through their nostrils. I believe that we each carry our own portion of goodness, and that when that spirit is passed from one to another, by a glance or a smile, the totality of good grows in proportions that we can't comprehend. There is truth in the adage "The Kingdom of God is within you!" Take a look, says I! Try a spiritual MRI!

My doctor tells me that if I don't drink or smoke, and if I eat food that is good for me, I'll die a relatively healthy man. And one nice thing about death is the absolute certainty of a last laugh. Still, as I draw closer to that fateful day, my perception of what comes after is not clear at all. I once met a Benedictine monk named Father Basil who told me that there's another life after this and that when I reach it the only question the deity will ask me is, "Did you have a good time?"

Unequivocally I can say yes, yes I did.

All I know for sure is that when I go, I'm not going to be "laid to rest." When I think about this old bod of mine being pressed under six feet of sod, or incinerated into flakes and fragments, or even shoved off on a raft into the freezing Arctic sea, *laid to rest* aren't the first words that come to mind.

Nor do I expect to pass away, or pass on, or cross over, or make the supreme sacrifice, or come to an untidy end; it's not likely I'll meet my maker or go to my eternal reward. I'm not going to breathe my last, bite the dust, kick the bucket, buy the farm, or take the dirt nap; I'm not going to turn up my toes, join the silent majority, become a landowner, push up daisies, play a harp, take a taxi, give up the ghost, feed the worms, enter the sweet hereafter, shuffle off the mortal coil, or any other of the convenient clichés that try to sidestep the reality.

I plan to die.

But before I do, I have a few more things to explore.

So read on, dear children.

# ONE

# Angela's Diary

*Because I could not stop for Death,*
*He kindly stopped for me;*
*The carriage held but just ourselves*
*And Immortality.*

EMILY DICKINSON

Death has always been a particularly confusing situation for the Irish. We're the only race that celebrates the wake and mourns the marriage. With beliefs rooted in pagan times, a healthy dose of guilt, shame, and misinformation courtesy of Holy Mother Church, and perhaps a jar or two too much of liquid spirits, it's no wonder we don't know which way is up, or down, as it were, when it comes to how we're supposed to die, and what happens after.

Right from the first, death had me scratching the old cranium.

———

As far as I can gather, the father and his father came to America in 1922 to escape the vengeance of His Majesty's law lads for activities against the interests of the Crown. Although IRA membership and purported heroism increase with the number of downed pints in Ireland, the talk was that grandfather was wanted for the dispatching of a constable of the RIC, the Royal Irish Constabulary. There was a letter, one that hung around for years, a very official-looking one in that grave organized-rebellion way, that asked for safe conduct to America for the duo. The father remained here; the grandfather returned to Ireland after the hunt had been called off.

Or so the story goes.

Malachy Sr. then met up with the mother, Angela, in 1930 at a dance in Brooklyn, after which they did what most of us cannot imagine our parents doing. The result of the "knee trembler," what the smart Irish call stand-up sex against a wall, was pregnancy, and thus began the gallop of Angela's family folk, mostly large female cousins from Brooklyn, and husbands thereof, to the rescue. The daddy was made to marry the mammy. No shotguns present, just a stern Irish warning of the punishment to come if Daddy declined. For if the Jews have a monopoly on guilt, then the Irish RCs own the monopoly on remorse. (Protestants have regrets only, thank you.)

Five months later, on August 19, 1930, there popped out in Brooklyn, America, that literary lad Frank McCourt. A year, a month, and a day later it was my turn to pop out, on September 20, 1931, and a year and a month after that out popped the twins, Eugene and Oliver, not identical but very much together in mischief and mirth. A year later, in the midst of the five males and the mother, there popped out Margaret Mary McCourt. Five children in a little over four years and the rhythm method be damned.

If the last of the American McCourts had been a male, I doubt I would remember Margaret Mary the way I do, but a male she wasn't. Instead the most exquisite angelic entrancing little creature with amazing black hair, the bluest of blue eyes, and baby skin that was so pure it was almost translucent have a permanent place in my mind. Her little voice sent out a sound so softly musical that we didn't mind at all if she cried.

In my memory, illuminated by the arrival of this tiny magical being, the shabby apartment was suddenly filled with song, smile, and loving talk as we crowded around her crib just to look at her.

Frank, Oliver, Eugene, and I all slept in the same bed, twins at the bottom, Frank and I at the head of the bed with me on the inside. There was a severe shortage of sheets, so changes of bedclothes were infrequent, and the immediate atmosphere around our bed could be described as acrid. We were not piss poor; there was more than enough to go around.

Then crash! The light of life, love, and laughter flickered and went out.

It was the anguished voice of my father that awakened me that night, and when my eyes adjusted, they were filled with the sight of him standing in the middle of the room, outlined against the light-lit doorway with his shadow enlarged on the wall. For some reason his arms were outstretched, and he was holding Margaret Mary in his hands, from which she drooped like a rag doll. I could see the shadow of her head, her arms, her legs that just hung limply, silently in the shadowed room. My father just kept repeating the same words: "God blast it to hell! God blast it to hell," which was unusual for him, as he was a bit prudish about what he called bad language and, when sober, was the quietest man you could imagine.

He was sober then, and he left the room carrying my sister, with the apartment walls absorbing the ancient keening wail of a bereft mother. The terror of the unknown paralyzing me even to the vocal cords, I couldn't even ask, "What's happening?" and I couldn't even move to go and find out. Angela was moaning, "Oh, Jesus, Mary, and holy Saint Joseph, what have you done to me? Why have you taken my child? Blast you. Blast you. Blast you."

I lay in the bed, afraid to move, my brothers not stirring for some reason. Was I the only one aware? In the morning we got up, and the mother was in the kitchen buttering some bread and boiling the kettle for some tea, which were our breakfast. The dad was absent and so was Margaret Mary; the mother explained he had taken her to the hospital to see the doctor.

The father returned. MM did not.

The little voice disappeared from our lives, and the explanation given by the father was that the angels had taken her to heaven, where she was very happy playing all day on swings and seesaws.

The mother then fell into a darkness. She sat staring into space, not paying much attention to us, no food, and sometimes we sat and watched as the ash on her cigarette grew longer, longer, fascinating us and making us wonder when it would fall.

In memory the ash never does fall. The smoke rises and rises forever, and the mother's eyes stare forever into space.

In today's psychology, Mam would have been diagnosed with a severe postpartum depression complicated by grief, but back then her condition came from the weight of a world too cruel to carry. Undiagnosed and untreated, the mother's condition was handled the only way her cousins who lived in Brooklyn knew how.

They sent her home to Ireland—and us along with her.

Ahead lay the years in Ireland the brother Frank so famously chronicled. The poverty and wretched conditions smothered us, but not so much as to extinguish the memory of Margaret Mary or the question of her whereabouts.

The frequent queries to the mother elicited a blank stare and a halting, "The doctor took her away."

"To where?" we asked.

"The hospital, I think," she said.

"But when is she coming back?"

"I don't know. Stop bothering me," the mother said. We tormented her with that sort of question until she'd explode in anger, and tell us to shut up and leave her alone.

And so my first experience with death was the perfect first stage of grief in the Kübler-Ross model: denial.

As it turned out, in the McCourt family you could deny a death for a very long time. Years later, in her diary, the mother would finally put pen to paper to express the reality of her grief:

> When the baby girl was three weeks old, we found her dead in her crib. From there on, I fell to pieces. I got a nervous breakdown and, my God, what a time I had. I didn't know if it was night or day, and to make things worse, Malachy McCourt went off to get drunk, just to drown his sorrows.

But when I was a child, the repudiation of Margaret Mary's death left me in a state of suspended animation. You don't know what the fuck is going on. And so my views on death were screwed up from the very beginning. There was no completion of the stages of grief. It was either a seesaw with baby Jesus or the longest extended hospital stay in the history of mankind. It was all very mysterious and confusing, like parents trying to explain how babies are conceived and born. And yet somehow the questions about Margaret Mary that seemed so important faded into embers and became lodged in the dark recesses of my mind.

It would be about sixty years before the answer came. My son Conor had become a police officer in the New York Police Department, and he used his talents and connections to try to track down the grave of Margaret Mary, if indeed there was such a grave. There was! She was buried alongside twenty-three other children of indigent families who couldn't afford individual plots. The mass grave was in St. John Cemetery in Queens, New York, which is the world capital of dead people, as there are more than four times as many people in the ground of that borough as there are walking the streets. One family had generously erected a monument with slots to enable each of the families to slide in a plaque bearing the name of their child to mark the place of interment.

So came the day in 1997 when the tribe McCourt trekked to St. John Cemetery, Queens, New York, to finally memorialize and mark the ground where the baby bones of Margaret Mary lay buried. There were Frank and Ellen, Mike and Joan, Alphie and Lynn, Diana and myself, my sons Conor and Cormac, and grandchildren gathered around. My wife, Diana, had kept some of Angela's famous ashes, and we scattered them on Margaret Mary's little grave. It was here that my old Catholic indoctrination kicked in. In my imagination this angel was in the bleakness of nowhere lonely and distressed. She was floating through the darkness wondering if there was a love anywhere, trying to see through the impenetrable mists and rain, crying out in the permanent fog for her mother or someone to hold her, hug her, and tell her she was loved. Year after year she wandered in the cold stygian nothingness encountering nothing, nobody, total oblivion. Then one day a door opened, and suddenly her life after death was flooded with sunshine and there on the other side were her brothers and their children and her mother smiling in warm greeting. As her mother's ashes came floating down on the grave she was gathered in her mother's arms and away they went into the soft sunlight of another caring world as I recited, with a slight shift of pronoun, this beautiful poem by Yeats:

Away with us she's going,
The solemn-eyed:
She'll hear no more the lowing
Of the calves on the warm hillside
Or the kettle on the hob
Sing peace into her breast,
Or see the brown mice bob
Round and round the oatmeal chest.
For she comes, the human child,
To the waters and the wild
With a faery, hand in hand,
For the world's more full of weeping than she can
    understand.

# TWO

# Christmas in Limerick

*A new servant maid named Maria*
*Had trouble lighting the fire*
*The wood being green*
*She used gasoline*
*Her position now is much higher*

There's a legend of sorts in Limerick, Ireland, about a saint named Munchin who sometime in the sixth century took to building a church in town. One day his workmen came upon a heavy stone that they couldn't lift. Munchin asked some of the townspeople for assistance, but they refused. Luckily for the saint, a group of Nordic strangers happened by and helped put the stone in its place. Afterward Saint Munchin prayed that the strangers would flourish in Limerick and that the natives would perish, or at least have a very hard time. As was the case with many a pious Irishman who followed, old Munchin knew how to hold a grudge. And so the Curse of Saint Munchin began and was soon preserved in verse, part of which reads:

Saint Munchin was pleased with the job,
And he laughed with devout satisfaction;
Then he gave every stranger a bob
Along with his best benediction.
"May strangers henceforward!" he cried,
"In Limerick fast prosper and flourish;
While, like the bad froth of the tide,
The Natives will dwindle and perish,
With plenty of nothing to do!"
Thus, from that day to this, 'tis well known
How strangers in Limerick are thriving;
While the natives all backward are thrown,
Or headlong to ruin are driving!
Och, troth, 'twas a very droll stone,
To cause them so bitter a luncheon;
Filched, fleeced, starved, and stripped to the bone,
By the curse of the blessed Saint Munchin.

I don't know how Saint Munchin's blessing on strangers missed us, but it did. Flourish we didn't. And prosper? Not the chance of a patch on my trousers.

———

As mentioned, Margaret Mary's death was the reason the McCourts left Brooklyn, America, and sailed to Ireland and, after a few unscheduled stops, settled in a town called Limerick, which then had cornered the market on death, destitution, and despair.

The voyage happened something like this: We piled our meager clothes into what they called a steamer trunk, and off we went to the big ship. That must have been 1934, and I have been told that the whole world was in a state of dark despair and depression even for people whose little sisters had not died. There was a fellow named Adolf Hitler over in Germany who had gotten himself the position of führer on the promise that he was going to make Germany great again. Americans, including the much-honored Charles Lindbergh, the motorcar magnate Henry Ford, whose photo Hitler kept in his office, and a man named Fred Koch, who built some oil refineries for the Nazis, much admired him. And then there was a man named Thomas Watson, whose company IBM helped with the statistical problems of transporting Jews to concentration camps and killing them. He got a special medal from Hitler that he returned after several years of consideration, during which time several million Jews were exterminated. As far as I know, none of the Jews who were killed were given or returned any medals. There were also groups of ordinary Americans who supported Hitler, swept up no doubt in his talk of purity of race and white supremacy.

The McCourts, who headed for Ireland against the tide of Irish headed for America, knew nothing of this. We were adrift in a sea of hopelessness, sailing in the wake of Margaret Mary's death, the mother never to be right and whole again, and the father perhaps already plotting his escape with drink and distance. I don't know if the mother blamed America for MM's death or not. But I do believe she thought that in Ireland, God's grace would never have allowed such a thing to happen. That was the irony of our journey. For in Ireland,

God's grace would be in short supply, because death was no stranger to our family.

The voyage across the Atlantic, though, did excite us children. Frequently I performed a disappearing act, but Mother always knew where to find me: always in the crew quarters on top of a table, singing an old Irish song for bread:

> The Garden of Eden has vanished, they say
> But I know the lie of it still;
> Just turn to the left at the bridge of Finnea
> And stop when halfway to Cootehill.
> 'Tis there I will find it, I know sure enough
> When fortune has come to me call,
> Oh, the grass it is green around Ballyjamesduff
> And the blue sky is over it all.
> And tones that are tender and tones that are gruff
> Are whispering over the sea,
> Come back, Paddy Reilly, to Ballyjamesduff
> Come home, Paddy Reilly, to me.

George Bernard Shaw once said that the USA and Great Britain were two countries divided by a common language. In the USA, when they called me *cute* it had to do with the fact that I was blond and blue-eyed, with perfect little white teeth, and with the kind of complexion that was the desire of many a woman. I was also energetic, quick to smile, and polite.

In Ireland, *cute* is not exactly what I just described, nor is it a compliment. The various meanings are all pejorative and include cunning, devious, manipulative, charmingly criminal, and deceitful. The Irish *cute* is also often coupled with another unflattering word so as to be more descriptive, which the Irish like to be. One of the most common examples of this compound phrasing is *cute hoor*, which is applied to many of our native Irish politicians, who will not only take your money but try to convince you that they are pleasuring you in the process. Now *hoor*, of course, is the Irish way of pronouncing *whore*. Whilst I was not old enough to be a cute hoor, I was always in need of something and was not averse to sharing my talents, as it were, for a couple of sweets or biscuits, jam and bread, or, of course, money. And as I was cute as defined on both sides of the Atlantic, I wasn't averse, given the opportunity, to swiping little items whenever I could. The only thing missing from my charming possessions was the wings, and perhaps a tail and horns. My father took to calling me Boldy.

I was sorry to have to leave the sea, the ship, and all my crew pals who loaded me down with fruit, sweets, and pennies. I would have been much sorrier had I known how thin the menu was where we were headed. But off we were, on a bus to the father's home, a town in Antrim, Northern Ireland, called Toome Bridge:

> O see the fleet-foot host of men, who march with faces
>    drawn,
> From farmstead and from thresher's cot, along the
>    banks of Ban;
> They come with vengeance in their eyes. Too late!
>    Too late are they,
> For young Roddy McCorley goes to die on the bridge
>    of Toome today.

ETHNA CARBERY

Grandpa and Grandma McCourt greeted this invasion of bodies from America—Dad, Mam, Frank, Malachy, Eugene, and Oliver—somewhat stonily, and the magical cunning charm of me did not seem to work in the puritanical North. Even the Catholics there behaved like Presbyterians. Respectability, propriety, piety, and suffering were the order of the day, and laughter seemed a breach of civilization. The elders had long discussions about what was to become of us, and the prevailing opinion was, whatever we did, we were not welcome to dwell in the grandparents' house, and we should get ourselves south to the Irish Free State, where my mother's family lived. There my father might get a job, but there was nothing for Catholics in the occupied territory.

Once more we packed and loaded ourselves onto a bus, and off we were to a place called Dublin, which was about a hundred miles away. We arrived in the free Irish capital too late for the train to Limerick. There was no money for a hotel, or other lodging, for that matter, and if it weren't for the kindness of the Garda Síochána, the Irish police, we would have ended up walking the streets broad and narrow just like the ghost of Molly Malone.

> In Dublin's fair city,
> Where the girls are so pretty,
> I first set my eyes on sweet Molly Malone,
> As she wheeled her wheelbarrow,
> Through streets broad and narrow,
> Crying, "Cockles and mussels, alive, alive, oh!"

No cockles or mussels for us. Instead we spent the night behind bars as guests of the kindly guards who were entertained to no end by the four Yank kids "wit' da" Brooklyn accents, although I've never spoken like that in my life.

Again I sang "Paddy Reilly," and again we were given sweets and jam and bread. This country was an easy mark, I thought. Oh, how wrong I was. I was taken with claustrophobia, though, when the lights dimmed, and the shadows of the bars fell long across the floor, and the clanging of the cell doors closing echoed in my ears. Even eighty years later I feel a cold chill at the remembrance of the sound.

The next day we were off to Limerick. There we would be welcomed. Of course we would:

City of churches and beautiful spires,
City of pubs and of lonely desires,
City of gossips that wait to be told,
City of youth that waits to grow old,
Society's city. Home of the snob,
Show me your penny before you hobnob.
Do have a coffee do have a bun.
Do what the others do cause it is done.

Outsiders who came to dwell in Limerick were classified as "blow-ins," and even after you'd lived there for a century or so the designation still followed you like the stink off a barrow of mussels. This insular nature of the Irish town affected the father more than us, the children. Children are much more progressive than adults, who are busy building walls to keep the "others" out, whoever the others are, and in Limerick my father was an "other" due to his birth in the North. You didn't have to come from so far away to feel the chill of otherness. There were nine main churches in Limerick, but only one of them was called "the parish," and that was Saint Mary's. The rest, Saint Joseph's, Saint Michael's, Our Lady of the Queen of Peace, Saint John's, and so on, were also-rans. If you were from "the parish" you were pure Limerick, which meant you were volatile, suspicious, and somewhat illiterate—in other words, Republican. They had a sign there that read "God bless the Pope in Saint Mary's Parish."

I remember one fellow from Saint Mary's who married an outsider and took a rental home across the Baal's Bridge in a nearby section of Limerick. When people from the parish talked about him, they'd say, "He moved across the water," as though he'd sailed the Atlantic Ocean. The Baal's Bridge spanned the Abbey, a tributary to the Shannon that was about twenty-two feet wide.

———————

In Limerick we were classified as "Laners," a pejorative term for those of us who lived in the fetid slum lanes of Limerick, the lowest form of life on this earth. The Malachy I remember from then was garbed in a gansey (a light woolen shirt with a small collar), short trousers, for some reason woolen stockings to the knee, and well-worn boots. The elbows of the gansey had long departed, as the poor have sharp bones and are without flesh to blunt the protruding edges that cut through clothing. With so many patches in evidence the trousers sometimes looked as if they had been fashioned from material cut from Joseph's coat of Biblical fame. The heels of the stockings rode up, displaying little edges of white flesh declaring that these leg coverings were in need of darning (black shoe polish did a good job of covering the flesh).

All these items could be described as begrimed, as I had no change of clothing to facilitate the washing of this one outfit. When the mother decided the stink of the body and its covering was too much and everything had to be cleaned, we were stripped and put in bed till all was washed and hung out to dry in the rainy Irish climate. Said drying sometimes took a day and a night. The stockings that heretofore had been able to stand without support were now soft and supple and pleasant to the feet. The short pants were now devoid of the caked shit on the inner back seam, and the gansey, cleared of the accumulation of grease on its front, could now be observed with its original color and pattern intact.

When Frank was six and made his first Holy Communion, I was five and extremely jealous because of the suit he got from the Society of Saint Vincent de Paul and the white armband and lapel medal he wore. I kicked up such a row that to make me quit they got a suit for me from the charity and somehow got me to believe I was part of his day. A first Communion is a coming-out party that makes you an official sinner, and the newly endowed then visits neighbors and relatives to be admired and to make the collection. After which it was off with the suit, back into the rags, and a gallop to O'Connell's Shop for the sweets and then a dash to the Lyric Cinema for a film. Frank took me along, and I think we watched Hopalong Cassidy on the screen.

There was a terrible shame in traversing the aisle of Saint Joseph's Church to kneel and receive the sacrament of Holy Communion. While the well-to-do in our community were in all their finery on Sundays (and yet managing to look humble in approaching the altar rails to receive the body and blood of Jesus Christ), the guttersnipes and ragamuffins like me had to slink as close to the ground as possible. No matter how we tried, however, the patches on patches sometimes parted to show the pink arse of a kneeling boy, and the position of kneeling, of course, showed the departed soles of the busted boot.

Along with the shame came an abundance of disappointment.

One Christmas season when I was about seven, I went wandering about the town of Limerick on my own, as was my wont. Festive holly, ivy, and even some sparkly lights festooned the shopwindows. What caught my roving eye, though, was the train in the window of Todd's, Limerick's department store. With a lovely engine, the train was complete with caboose, passenger carriages, and tiny people seated the window. It went around and around on tracks that passed through a tunnel in a mini mountain and by a train station complete with signals and little bursts of steam. As instructed, I tried to be a good boy and prayed that Santa Claus would bring me the train for Christmas. I managed to get downtown to Todd's daily to keep an eye on "my train." When I heard the Santa himself was going to make an appearance at Todd's to hear requests from the children I was off to present mine. Of course, as grimy and patched as I was, the man at the door to the store wouldn't let me in.

"Get your arse out of here," he told me.

Undeterred, I made my way to the Redemptorist church. The hell with the guy at the door, I thought, I was going right to the top man, or top child as it were.

I arrived at the church in the early evening. In the solemn darkness, I knelt on the marble step just outside the altar rail and in front of the nativity scene. As it was still before Christmas, the statue of the baby Jesus hadn't arrived yet, but I asked Mary and Joseph to ask Jesus to speak to Santa Claus for me, as Claus was the one who handled the deliveries. I prayed for the train until nearly nine, when a stern priest commanded me to leave, as they were closing for the night. I was sure my message had gotten through.

Christmas Day arrived on schedule and, along with my brothers, I crept down the creaky stairs filled with hope and expectation. It had to be there, I assured myself, I had done all that I was supposed to do, and I had never prayed for something so hard in my life. There was absolutely no reason that God and Santa wouldn't make good on their part of the bargain.

As poor as we were, there was no Christmas tree or stocking hung or roasted chestnuts; no wrapping paper, ribbon, or bows.

The only gift for me was a notebook for school.

I told this story to a journalist from upstate New York named Chuck Walley a few years back when he asked me what Christmas was like for me in Limerick.

A month or so later, Chuck called to tell me that he was going to be in New York City with his wife and son to do some Christmas shopping, and he asked if Diana and I would like to meet him at that marvelous restaurant the Oyster Bar in Grand Central Station for lunch. It sounded lovely. Diana and I got ourselves down to the rendezvous with Chuck and his family.

There is an annex of the New York Transit Museum in Grand Central Station that holds exhibits and sells train-related merchandise. Chuck asked if we minded stopping there first, as he was going to pick up a present for someone. So in we went, and the next thing I knew I was bathed in the light of cameras both still and television video, and surrounded by a group of people shouting Christmas greetings. A man introduced himself as a vice president of Lionel, the premier maker of toy trains in the world. He presented me with the latest state-of-the-art toy train.

I thought back on that seven-year-old kneeling on the cold marble in the dark church and began to cry. Was this now the answer to that prayer? Three-quarters of a century later? What does the train do for me now except bring tears? And yet how much fuller and more meaningful was getting the gift at eighty, having gone through all that I had?

Was my prayer answered? Maybe it was, or perhaps my receiving the train was just the product of a story told to a wonderful friend.

Believe what you want.

As the tears rolled down my face that day, I knew what I believed. Maybe because I received so little of it as a child, nothing moves me more than an act of kindness. Chuck's Christmas gesture was not, in my mind, about a baby born in a manger or an old guy with a white beard in a red suit, but about someone doing something thoughtful and selfless for someone else.

# THREE

# Finnegan's Wake

*"What a great country Ireland would be if
we spent half as much time on the living
as we do on the dead."*

MICHEÁL MACLIAMMÓIR,

IRISH ACTOR

Someone once asked what the death rate in Limerick was.
"Same as everywhere else," came the reply. "One per person."
It seemed more than that to me.

About eleven of our pals in school died between the ages
of six and ten years old, mostly from something we called the
"galloping consumption," a virulent form of tuberculosis. No
wonder. The school had one old hot water pipe running the
length of the wall, and that was the heat. Even a hearth fire
seemed cold and damp, fueled by peat, turf soaked for so long
in the Irish rain it never dried, or so it seemed.

But there were other causes common among the poor
and those who did not matter. There was Matty Heslin, who
drowned in the Shannon, and Mickey Kelly, who one day

tumbled down the steps by the bridge after his heart had given out. He died of poverty. Who had the money to have a kid's heart checked? There was Bonky Galvin, the one fat kid in all of the Limerick slum. Not fat from food, however, but a thyroid problem. He died at ten. There was a kid named Fitzpatrick who had a bad leg and limped. No shoes, freezing, little to eat in the school. He died of poverty too.

Galloping consumption took the rest.

It was customary to get a half day off from school to attend the funerals of our friends, so we hoped death and burial happened only on weekdays during the school year. There was also the added attraction of going to the house of the dead lad, because there were lashings of lemonade and biscuits and times when the neighbors put down their little glasses of porter and stout, which our sharp-eyed gang quickly guzzled. We had such a good time we simply could not wait for the next person to die. There was one time when a friend of ours wasn't sure of the address of the home holding the wake. He knocked on the door and asked, "Is this where the dead man lives?"

Frank used to say we belonged to the death-of-the-month club.

One day we were in the People's Park, kicking a ball manufactured from paper and twine. There Matty Heslin (when he was still alive) mentioned that his mother told him that Paddy O'Brien's mother said that Paddy was in a bad way with the galloping consumption, and though the date of his departure was presently unknown, the mother believed death would come soon.

Now, we all liked Paddy. He was a fine strapping lad of about eleven years of age who had proudly shown a bunch of us the beginnings of a small garden of pubic hair, and he was faster than any squirrel when climbing trees in the orchards from which we stole apples. But then the GC hit and down he went. Though we knew we would miss him, there was also the question of the timing of his demise. You see, it was in the middle of August when this occurred, a full two weeks to the beginning of school.

When discussing our friend's impending death, we decided that the eloquent brother Frank should visit Paddy and point out to him that we were still on summer holidays, et cetera. Frank had none of my natural ability to coerce and went about the world even in childhood with a face, to steal a line from Brendan Behan, that looked like a plateful of mortal sin. Throughout his childhood and beyond, brother Frank garnered designations including Cranky Franky, Thorny Wire, and Tantrum Thrower. The adage goes that you shouldn't judge a book by its cover. Frank spent his life masking the softness behind the facade he showed the world, a softness that his pen could not hide.

So Frank, who even at the age of nine was eloquent and literate, hied himself over to P. O'B.'s house. Mrs. O'Brien, the mother, greeted him at the door and was touched by his visit. As Frank described later, Paddy was in bed shrunken so much that he looked more like the last remaining victim of the Irish Famine than the big lad we knew. According to Frank, the following conversation took place:

**F.** How ya, Paddy.

**P.** (From collapsed cheeks) How ya, Frankie.

**F.** Do you know you are dying?

**P.** I don't.

**F.** Well, you are! Do you know we are still on our holidays?

**P.** I do know that.

**F.** You can't go dying in the middle of the summer.

**P.** I can't do anything about it.

**F.** If you die before we go back to school, I'll kill you.

**P.** All right, all right. Go 'way and stop tormenting me.

True to his word, Paddy didn't die until September 2, and we got the half day off and the lemonade and biscuits and pilfered sherry and would get the same over and over again at our other dead classmates' funerals.

————

There are many tales of how Irish wakes came to tradition status. Some say the Irish hold wakes so that the attendees can reassure themselves that they are still alive. Another explanation for the noisy revelry is that it's to make certain that the departed is indeed dead and not in a prolonged faint. When we were children, we amused ourselves with grim stories of people being buried and then exhumed to reveal deep indentations left from fingernails on the undersides of the coffin lids. Of course, the horror stories enthralled us so much we never thought to ask why they removed the coffin in the first place, or why they examined the underside of the lid. During the Famine they used coffins that had sliding bolts on the underside, so they could just hold the box over the grave and pull the bolt, and the body would drop into the hole in the earth. This way the coffin could be used again.

The practice of offering food and drink at the wake has its roots, no doubt, in the ancient Brehon law system, the rule of the realm in Ireland for a thousand years, in which hospitality ranked supreme. The Brehon laws were amazingly progressive for their time. Fosterage, for instance, was the responsibility of a parent to rear and educate a child according to regulations. Molding character and nurturing the intimate bonds of blood relationships were carried on well into young adulthood. In those distant days, they placed hospitals beside clean running water, with openings facing south to allow in the sunshine, centuries before Florence Nightingale. Land and food were set aside to care for the aged and disabled and the orphaned young. Criminals had to make restitution to those whom they had harmed. If caught, murderers had to work all their lives for the victim's family.

Of course, those wonderfully equitable laws all went out with the snakes when a patrician slave named Maewyn Succat, whom they called Patrick, returned to the Emerald Isle around 432 as bishop and brought with him the weight of organized religion, under which the progressive Brehon laws collapsed. He chased the snakes, who came to America and became conservatives.

The Irish of the Middle Ages were terrified of being labeled inhospitable. Under the law of hospitality, you were enjoined never to let a stranger pass your door without offering him the best of what you had in your larder. No leftovers or crusts of bread. Ingrained as it was, and to some degree prevailing to this day, this old code was agonizing for the Irish when the Great Hunger descended on their country in the 1840s. Inside many isolated cottages were women dying of starvation and children already dead and being gnawed by hungry rats, with the man of the house sitting and staring into the bleak, barren, dead countryside outside his door. And yet, even under that dire circumstance, a stranger would be welcomed to whatever little they might have. A stranger, it was thought then, could be a deity, or, more importantly, might say awful things about the place he had just passed through.

So how did alcohol become part of Irish hospitality?

Well, the word *whiskey* comes from the Gaelic word *uisce*, which means water, but the full phrase is *uisce beatha*, which is pronounced ISHKA BAHA and translates to "water of life." Now, you can make an alcoholic beverage out of anything, including a sweaty sock, which was readily available. Whiskey was probably the only item of worth a starving man could offer to a passing stranger.

Of course, once introduced, whiskey took on its own importance.

In James Joyce's *Finnegans Wake* there are dancing, singing, carousing, and a bit of fisticuffs, and someone has the temerity to bring a bottle of whiskey that smashes against the wall over the head of the dead one, splattering that valuable potion on all and sundry, including the face of the corpse, and what happens? Lo and behold there comes about a resurrection, which shows you the power of whiskey. It kills the living and revives the dead! And all that for the price of a dirty sock! No wonder it became customary, and no wonder it's referred to as spirits.

In those pagan times, mischief filled the Irish wake tradition. Unwitting mourners would have their shoelaces tied together, and older men would have their coats sewn to the chairs on which they sat. Often someone would sneak under the bed that held the corpse and shake it. Fights were often part of the evening. One story had it that a young man who'd just put his father in the grave turned to address the assembled mourners. "It's a sad day when my father is put in the clay, and not even one blow struck at his funeral," he said. With that he punched the man standing next to him, and so the fight began, and everyone went home happy.

In the last century, along with fights, storytelling, dancing, singing, and praying, some very strenuous game playing took place. They chose teams, and there were lifting competitions along with much pushing and shoving. Testosterone abounded, and not only in feats of strength. Priests devoted many a Sunday sermon to condemning the doings at Irish wakes and warned young women that they risked the loss of their virtue and immortal souls by attending these savage activities. The clergy also blamed alcohol for the more outrageous behavior and directed parishioners to wake the dead without any alcohol in the house. The response, as you might have guessed, was negative. Any versed wake-goer knows there are two essential elements for a wake: (1) a corpse and (2) alcohol. That's the way it was, and still is, as far as I know.

Another practice back then was to wreathe the departed's home in branches and leaves, the purpose of which was to disguise the house in case the dead had offended residents of the otherworld who might come back to take their revenge. In later years the bereaved family hung a funeral wreath on the door with a small card detailing the name, age, and gender of the dead one, and whatever funeral arrangements were in the offing.

These days it is typical for cars in a funeral motorcade to have their headlights on. This practice is the modern derivation of surrounding the coffin with candles in the old days. The flames, they thought, would frighten off evil spirits who might attempt to invade and occupy a body without the usual defenses against said invasion. It was also paramount, for the same reason, to get the body in the ground as soon as possible, and so today processions to cemeteries are allowed to speed their way through red lights and intersections.

The practice of women wearing a hat or veil did not begin out of reverence but the desire for a disguise, just in case the dead one uncovered a cache of sins the living spouse had committed.

Which reminds me of the joke my friend, the comedian Adrianne Tolsch, tells about the woman who has just turned forty and is walking across the street when she gets hit by a bus and killed. When she goes up to the pearly gates, she complains about dying so young.

"It was a mistake," Saint Peter says. "They happen."

So Saint Peter sends the woman back to earth, where she decides to take full advantage of her second chance. She goes to a plastic surgeon and has a facelift, a tummy tuck, and a boob job, and after all the surgeries, she looks ten years younger at least. Her first night out with her new looks, she steps into the street and gets hit by a bus.

"Again?" she says to Saint Peter at the gates.

"What do you want from me?" he says. "I didn't recognize you."

———————

In Limerick, Mrs. Moran is galloping down the lane. You can tell she carries vital news by the eager expression on her face. Her lips are pursed, her eyes open wide. If she doesn't tell someone soon, she surely will pull a muscle.

And here comes Mrs. Holland down the other way.

"Do you know who died?" says Mrs. Moran.

"Tell me who," comes the high-pitched reply.

"Mr. Patterson down the lane."

"Oh my God. What did he die of?"

"'Twas nothing serious."

"Thank God for that."

———————

The usual formula in the Limerick of my youth was that a couple of neighborhood women, like my aunt Aggie and her diminutive pal Mary Patterson, were called on to wash and shave the body and clothe it in the brown habit of the Third Order of Saint Francis. The dead person's clothing was given to relatives. I wore a suit that belonged to my dead uncle, Pa Keating, when I came back to America, and was grateful to have the threads.

Since there was usually a shortage of clean ones, the family borrowed sheets, and the corpse, now clean and spiffy in its new duds, was laid out in the bedroom. The original reasons for some of these practices are lost. Why do they wash the corpse, shave the face, and cut the nails? One account has it that the person who's dead is going to an audition, so to speak, and has to be presentable and clean and have no body odor offensive to the God Guy. I don't know about that.

People would then arrive with cakes, sweets, beverages, clay pipes, tobacco, and always snuff, and traditionally visitors knelt at the bedside to pray for the repose of the soul of the departed, or, if the newly dead owed them money, to make sure that he or she wasn't breathing. In the evening some of the more musically inclined folk would drop by and just so happen to have a fiddle or an accordion in their possession.

Horses drew the hearse that transported the dead. The priest's carriage was drawn by a white horse and traveled ahead of the hearse. You could have one, two, or four horses drawing the priest's carriage, depending on your ability to pay. If you were like us, you had barely enough for a priest to come to the house and mumble some Latin and sprinkle some holy water, and if you gave more he'd come to the graveyard. For the Church, death was the gift that kept on giving. The well-to-do would put up a fund for a novena of Masses to be said on the anniversary of their relative's death. There was constant talk of prayers for the repose of the soul, but it always cost pounds.

Of course, when it was all said and done, it was money and custom that determined the last service your loved ones had and, in some cases, how and when they would get into heaven.

Before Frank authored his famous memoirs, he wrote articles for the *Village Voice*, a left-leaning newspaper here in New York.

One of the articles was about an old man who told a somewhat romantic story of the existence of a Jewish princess buried in a Jewish cemetery out in a generally southerly direction from Limerick. There were no details offered of just how a person attains the status of a Jewish princess, but the old fellow did inform Frank that all Jews are buried standing up and with a five-pound note clutched in the right hand. The purpose, as the man said, is apparent. No Jews can get into heaven on merit, as some Christians believe, so they have to rely on guile and bribery, he said. Being buried standing up gives them a running start on the last day, and the five-pound note slipped into Saint Peter's hand ensures swift entry to a comfortable seat at the right hand of Himself.

It is extremely doubtful that the story has any veracity at all. Word of buried five-pound notes would have traveled very quickly through the lanes of Limerick, and hordes with shovels would have stormed the graveyard, not unlike the mob that went after Frankenstein's monster.

In Belfast in 1705, thieves unearthed the coffin of Margorie McCall, who had been buried wearing a very expensive ring. As the grave robbers tried to cut the Lady McCall's finger off, she awoke from her coma. It is said that when she returned home, her husband fainted. McCall lived for several years longer, and when she finally died for good, they buried her in the same plot in Shankill Graveyard with a headstone that read, "Margie McCall, Lived Once, Buried Twice."

Grave robbing is not the sovereignty of only the Irish. Curse or no curse, many a pharaoh was still warm in his tomb when looters ransacked. Grave robbers stole Charlie Chaplin's body out of his three-hundred-pound coffin and held it for a ransom of £400,000. Chaplin's wife, Lady Oona Chaplin, who was the playwright Eugene O'Neill's daughter, refused to pay the ransom, saying that Charlie would have thought it ridiculous. The funny man had very deep pockets and very short arms, and was known for never picking up a dinner check. Police captured the grave robbers, who led them to the star's remains, buried in a cornfield ten miles from the cemetery.

There was a time not too long ago when wakes in Limerick and, generally speaking, in all of Ireland had an assembly of women who took turns outlining the qualities of the dead man or woman, usually in a high-pitched tone and with rhythmic words that were carefully phrased so as not to stumble upon a character defect, no matter how plentiful they might have been. There was no hesitation in bestowing the most divine virtues on even the vilest characters. The practice was known as keening, and the mourners were known as keeners.

Here's an example of what you might hear from a keener:

"A grand man he was with a smile for all on his friendly face and his hand in his pocket at all times pulling out the pence to give to the poor or a deprived child. Ochone, ochone, ochone. He had the comforting word for the bereaved, and there was not a moment in his life that he was not offering a prayer for the suffering with a special devotion to the Virgin Mary that she might intercede with her Son to heal those near death. He has gone to his rest now but not for long because he will be up and about helping the good Lord in the work of caring for the poor on earth. Ochone, ochone, ochone."

As with most occupations, the best keeners were those who could improvise and separate themselves from the crowd. Such was the case with a great character in town whose name was Ghurki McMahon. We called him Ghurki because he claimed he'd once belonged to the famous Gurkha regiment in the Indian Army, which fought with the motto "Better to die in battle than live a coward."

It would have been difficult for Ghurki to utter those words in battle, seeing as he never left Ireland in his life and I know of no battle the Gurkhas fought in Limerick. Your man, however, did have a reverence for the dead and did not miss a single wake or funeral in Limerick, regardless of whether he knew the deceased, or the family of the deceased, or anyone even remotely related to the deceased.

Women usually did the keening, but Ghurki never hesitated to express thoughts that got him the liquid reward. Ghurki employed a conversational tone; being the gifted storyteller he was, he did not have to rely on dramatic intonation. No, Ghurki let the words speak for themselves. But what truly separated Ghurki from the pack was his remarkable ability to turn anyone's story into a story about himself. Below is an example:

"A grand man Padraig was, with a pair of shoulders on him so wide that he had to enter the doorway sideways—his shoulders were bruised from him trying to come in the door like an ordinary man. He could drink ten imperial pints of porter, and the intake would have no more effect on him than a cup of tea. A friend to every man and, if truth be told, there were many women who regretted their marriages when they were in his company. Yes, there were rumors about him and the sheep when he worked on the farm but I, for one, never believed them. Wasn't I at sea with him myself? I remember being on one of those Yankee sailing ships and swooping around Cape Horn and the captain saying to me there is a big storm gathering steam so get your arse up to the top of that mast and light the storm lantern. Aye, aye, sez I, because if I had said no, he'd hang me from that same mast, him being an Englishman plus a born-again Christian. So hand over fist I climbed that mast and just as I was lighting the lantern a great storm had come roaring out of the south pole obliterating the face of the moon—you could not see the moon for love or sausages—and the wind was howling like a banshee, and it was time for me to get down but before I was a third of the way, a great blast of wind whirled all the sails away into the blackness of the night like poor souls being sucked into damnation. The mast was now bucking back and forth like a demented horse, and the wind was coming this way and the waves slapping the boat like an old nun, and I was trying to hold on desperately wrapped like a toddler around his mother's leg. I got down to the bottom of the mast and there I found the mighty ship gone. Gone!"

Only once did Ghurki find himself bereft of words. Throughout the entire wake and funeral, he stayed quiet. Then, at the cemetery, the priest took a handful of dirt and threw it into the open grave.

"Ashes to ashes, dust to dust," the priest uttered. "If the Lord won't have you, the devil must."

All eyes turned to Ghurki, for the assembled found it hard to believe his silence.

"I couldn't have said it any better myself," our man said with a shrug.

Though wakes were an art form in Limerick and Ireland as a whole, one thing the Ireland of my day did not partake in with any regularity was murder. I believe there were only about two murders a year in all of Ireland when I was a child, and I was witness to the immediate aftermath of one of them.

Though my memory is hazy at best about the incident—I don't think I was much older than five or six—a man came staggering out of an alleyway clutching at his chest in an attempt to stop the blood that was running out of him. The man's murderer was captured, tried, and hanged.

All hangings in Ireland were conducted in a place paradoxically named Mountjoy Prison in Dublin. The hangman came from England, of course, as the Brits have eight centuries of experience in killing Irish. His name was Albert Pierrepoint, and he owned a pub called Help the Poor Struggler. The hangman had a methodical approach to his side job. He would unobtrusively size up the weight of the condemned and, just by looking, be able to estimate the length of rope he would need to snap the poor bugger's neck.

Everybody has to be good at something.

# FOUR

# The Roman Collar

*There was a young fellow from Tyne*
*Who put his head on the southeastern line*
*But he died of ennui*
*Because the five forty-three*
*Came in at a quarter to nine.*

All literary careers begin with the reading of books. And although Frank's and mine, and Alphie's too, would be many years in the making, the spark of enlightenment would begin in the Limerick of my youth.

When the father got the Irish divorce, which means he disappeared into England, it fell to Frank to take the paternal reins. So take them he did. The brother was a smallish fellow with brown eyes, black hair, and a sallow complexion like the father, and there was always a suspicion, in the Limerick of my day, that Protestant blood lurked in him, because of his looks and the fact of the father coming from County Antrim in the North. Frank had rheumy eyes that had to be practically boiled open every morning, and once they were there was bread to be gotten and the milk and tea for our sumptuous breakfasts, and we had to be scooted off to school. When he joined the Saint Joseph's 10th Limerick Troop, Catholic Boy Scouts of Ireland—and yes, there were Boy Scouts in Ireland even before America established them—Frank quickly became a leader.

A photo of Frank and me exists from that time that shows us with the neckerchief and the broad-brimmed hats. Along with the jaunty outfit, the life-changing part of the Scouts was the little library set up by Jack Brosnahan and Willie Loughlin. It was in that small room filled with donated books that the brother and I discovered the best and wittiest writer in the English language, P. G. Wodehouse, a man who convulsed us by satirizing the doings of the British upper classes. Loony and marvelous stories.

Many years later, in the 1950s, after I'd moved back to New York, I looked Wodehouse up. The New York telephone directory listed his address as 1000 Park Avenue. "Would that be possible?" I wondered. "A man of his standing in the telephone book?" I wrote a letter telling him how he had saved my brother and me from ignorance and illiteracy, and that an Englishman could do that for two Irish slum kids was beyond me. But you did, I said.

A few weeks later, I received a note from the great man. "Thank you very much," he wrote. "I'm glad you like my writing, but there is very little I can teach the Irish about literature."

The humility of his statement remains with me to this day.

The spark of enlightenment became a flicker, then a flame, with the opening of the Carnegie library in Limerick.

At the end of his days, the very wealthy Scotsman Andrew Carnegie decided to sell all his assets in steel and railroads and sponsor libraries. As Carnegie liked to say, "The man who dies rich dies a disgraced death." He endowed libraries around the world, and built some sixty of them in Ireland in the early nineteen hundreds. The Limerick Museum housed the Carnegie library. Chartered in the eleventh century, Limerick is rich in history and deserves a museum, as it was the site of a plethora of sieges, and it contains remnants of at least that many conquering armies, including that of our close friends and neighbors the British. And we the guttersnipes of Limerick deserved the library, even though the people who worked there despised us "dirty little Laners" and discouraged us from entering the sacred portals. When Frank and I discovered the library we were agog. Agog. Here was a room a little bigger than the average living room and filled with what we believed must be all the books in the whole world. We not only read the books, we ate them. The words they contained transported us from our miserable existence to exotic places inhabited by the most interesting, funny, and intelligent people.

And I read amazing stuff. My father had much respect for Pope Leo XIII. "A great friend of the workingman," he said. A drawing of Leo moved with us from America to Ireland and into all the slum houses afterward.

I read Leo's encyclical *Rerum novarum* cover to cover, and also *Das Kapital* by Karl Marx, both about the rights of the working class. I read *Mein Kampf*, an English version that then was unheard of. I don't know why it was there in the library or how I found it, though we did have a coterie of Nazis in

Ireland at the time. I inhaled the words on the page. I didn't know if I was a Catholic, a communist, a capitalist, or a complete nutcase, but I knew one thing for certain: I loved to read.

My taste in literature wasn't only for weighty political tomes. Oh no. I swallowed whole a bookshelf of cozies and whodunits and suspense novels and thrillers and other lighter fare. And there was always the tasty P. G. Wodehouse.

You can imagine then how devastated I was when the library banished me. Though later in my life I would be barred from a number of establishments, most of them in the business of selling spirits, in this particular case I was truly an innocent victim. And the punishment of not being able to use the library nearly broke my heart. The story went like this:

You had to get a library card, which cost two pennies. For two pennies you could get a pint of milk, which was practically sacred. Somehow we managed to pay the entry fee. If you were late returning a book, the fine was three pennies, so we were never late. If you lost the book, however, the fine was twelve shillings, which was at that time about what my mother was getting each week on the dole, or welfare—an unobtainable sum for a ten-year-old from the Lanes.

I forget the title of the book I was reading, but it was of great interest to a school pal named Val Gannon who asked to borrow it. Gannon had a tubercular leg, but that's not the reason I will never forget him. I lent him the book only after making it clear that it was from the library and that he'd have to be sure to give it back. I saw him a few days later, and he told me that he'd lost the book. A lie. He didn't lose the book. He sold it, no doubt for a cup. I couldn't pay the fine, of course, and so they wouldn't give me any more books. It was awful. After the longest year of my life, I sneaked in using another name and the librarian didn't recognize me. They didn't look twice at us slum kids, who were all alike, snotty and smelling and dirty. Val Gannon died not too long after, and I think he must be under a pile of burning overdue library books somewhere.

During the year of banishment, I didn't stop reading. Frank would take out a book, which we would take turns reading.

Frank had a very dominant personality and could terrorize other children and adults alike. He could indeed terrorize me, and with just a glance from those suddenly hard brown eyes of his. A more fearless kid did not exist in Ireland. Fists, feet, and tongue were his weapons. Opponents' weight and size were of no concern. Though Frank was small in stature and much slighter than I growing up (and in adulthood), I was careful not to arouse his wrath. Brothers are brothers, however, and since Cain-and-Abel, fights between them occur. So this one time we're in a bloody row over something now forgotten and Frank, of course, is getting the better of me. At some point I made the tactical decision to retreat. Retreat I did, but as I've already mentioned, I'm pretty cute when I need to be. And at that point I really needed to be.

Both of us loved British mystery books. Writers like G. K. Chesterton, W. Somerset Maugham, and Edgar Wallace set us ablaze. At the time I had just finished a Wallace mystery, and Frank had just begun it.

As I remember, the story concerns a police commissioner

and a few detectives who are investigating a murder in a house, when another murder occurs. How could the homicide have happened with only constables being in the house? Well, it turned out that the police commissioner had an identical twin brother who had kidnapped him, assumed his identity, and committed the murder. Crackling good tale. And that's where I had Frank. Soon as I reached the top of the lane, I turned and yelled: "The murderer is the police commissioner's identical twin brother!"

I could see the steam coming out of his ears, and so I made myself scarce for a couple of days until his blood came down from the boil.

———————

What were perhaps the first McCourt memoirs, at least for public consumption, began many years later, around 1977, at a party in the living room of friends Sheila and Brian Brown. Brian was a reporter and writer for *Time* magazine, and our kids went to the same schools. It was at the Browns' that Frank and I put a couple of scarves over our heads and began imitating the women from the lanes of Limerick of our youth.

Toothless, the women of the lanes would fling their black shawls about their shoulders like matadors as they faced each other in mortal verbal battle, for example:

"There are some in this lane who claim their husband was wounded in the war. Wounded he was. While running from the enemy, the backs of his legs being penetrated by his own hard balls of shit."

We had everyone laughing. Later Diana suggested we write down the material for a performance. So we jotted down a few of the stories. A fellow we knew named Mossie Cooney had a bar with a performance space upstairs that he called the Billy Munk Theater. Our props consisted of a table with newspaper as a tablecloth and two chairs, just as we'd had in our house in Limerick. We strung a few sketches together and got laughs again, this time in front of a larger audience that had paid to get in.

The performance at Billy Munk's wasn't our first time onstage. When Frank and I were about six or seven we decided to raise funds for the black babies in Africa. For some reason we believed that if we came up with enough money, a black baby would be given to us, which would make us the envy of all our neighbors. Someone nearby discarded some lengths of galvanized iron, which we hauled to the back room of our slum dwelling. We then secured some old buckets from the dump and fashioned the material into what we called a stage, which squeaked and groaned when we stepped upon it. Nevertheless, Frank decided the show would go on, and powdered lemonade would be available to the audience for a halfpenny a cup, and admission would be one penny. The performance itself consisted of Frank riding me piggyback and singing a cowboy dirge about how lonely it is out on the range. Along with having them pay admission, we expected the audience to get up onstage and sing along. The show ended abruptly when a small child leaped onto the stage, causing a complete collapse of the structure, which we couldn't get back together again. The whole venture realized two pennies for the black babies, not enough to buy one of our own but gratefully received by the Holy Ghost Missions to Africa.

At Billy Munk's we called our appearance (it wasn't a formal play yet) *A Couple of Blaguards*. *Blaguards* is a disparaging term coined first, it is said, by Jonathan Swift, who used "black guard" to describe Dublin dockworkers who unloaded English coal ships. They were hardworking laborers who drank, got rowdy, and sometimes fought, so the phrase was corrupted in a Dublinese way to *blaguards*. Grown-ups in Ireland got in the habit of referring to miscreant children as little blaguards, which the McCourt children were often called even by our grandmother.

Though it was first performed in 1977, we didn't write *Blaguards* until 1984. I was working on *Ryan's Hope*, a soap opera, and Frank was teaching at Stuyvesant High School. As always, we had our detractors. One of them was fairly well known to us. One night at a performance she stood in the audience to voice her displeasure.

"It's all a pack of lies," the mother yelled. "It wasn't that way atall."

I suggested that she come up and tell her side.

"I will not," she said. "I wouldn't be seen onstage with the likes of ye. I have a good name to maintain."

We had no idea, of course, that this slice of Limerick slum life would lead to an astonishing series of adventures around the world and beyond. As one Irish politician said, *Blaguards* was the first rolling stone in what would become an avalanche of McCourt memoirs. We went on to perform *Blaguards* hundreds of times around the country, including in San Francisco, where we played for seven weeks, and in Chicago, where the play ran for over a year. We even brought it to Limerick.

One of the great joys of my life was making brother Frank laugh. His was the most contagious laugh of anyone I'd ever known. One night in Chicago he was doing a piece of the show by himself. The sight of a ginger cat that had wandered onstage behind Frank's back and was performing his ablutions had convulsed the audience. The brother thought he must be particularly on that night until he turned around and saw the cat. I came onstage and said, "Frank, is that your pussy?" a line that elicited howls of laughter from the audience, Frank, the stage manager, and me, laughter that did not subside for at least fifteen minutes.

Frank was already writing at the time, and had published a few pieces in the *Village Voice* that were very well received. Jimmy Breslin, the columnist and author, said he was a marvelous writer, and told various people. Around that time somebody had said to me, someone from a publishing company, "You should write a book," and I said, "I'm not a writer, I'm a talker." When I told Frank about the conversation he said, "Why don't you?" And I said, "Because I think you should, you're the one with the story, and if you don't write our story I will, and I'll fuck it up, and you won't be able to write it again because once it's done it's done."

I didn't know it yet, but I was more than a talker. And the first time I put pen to paper for a story something magical happened. I don't mean to sound as if I'm some type of genius or something. I'm not. It's that when fresh ink is mixed with emotion long locked away in some dark corner of your mind, the result can set you free from the pain you carry. One day, in the beginning of the process that produced *Blaguards*, I was home expressing to Diana my desire to write, and she suggested that I try something simple to start. "Think of an experience you felt in a deep way," she said.

And so I took out the fountain pen and in earnest composed a story on the page for the first time:

"The sun streamed in the big window right on the bed with Oliver in it. Everything was white: Oliver's face, hair, his hands holding the baby rosary beads, the pillowcase, the sheets, the little white habit, all so bright you could hardly see him. Then a long smelly man came into the room, nodded to my father and took a piece of string out of his pocket and measured Oliver from head to toe and off he went.

"Me: Dad, what was the smelly man doing to Ollie?

"Dad: Shush. Oliver is gone off to heaven to play with the baby Jesus.

"Me: Will I have to go to heaven to play with the baby Jesus?

"Dad: No, we'll just kneel down and pray that Oliver is happy in heaven.

"I couldn't think of a prayer so I shook him and whispered, Wake up Ollie, wake up and we'll play horsey. He took no notice of me, so I tickled him. Tickle, tickle, tickle. Ollie wake up.

"The next thing I felt was a thump on the side of my head. I turned to see my grandmother standing there.

"'I'll give you tickle, tickle, you little blaguard,' she seethed. 'I'll give you who began it for disturbing the dead.'

"I ran out and hid under the stairs thinking that if heaven was such a great place why didn't my grandmother scoot off there and not be bothering me?

"When I heard her leaving, I came back in. Not long after that, the smelly man returned with the mother and Frankie. The smelly man was carrying a white box that had brass handles on it. He put it down on the floor and took the cover off and then he and the father lifted Oliver off the bed and put him in the box. That started the mother keening, moaning again, 'Oh sweet Jesus don't take him. Oh God, don't do this to me.'

"The father had to pull her back so the smelly man could put the cover on and he clamped it down with brass screws that had heads in the shape of crosses. He and the father carried the box outside followed by Frankie and myself dressed in our Sunday suits. Outside there was a big black carriage drawn by a lovely white horse and inside was the white box with Oliver laid across the long seat. We got in and set off down the lane, feeling very proud riding in that carriage and looking out the window hoping that all our pals would see us but they are never around when you want them. When the carriage stopped, we were in an old overgrown graveyard with old tombstones falling and leaning drunkenly waiting to be steadied. My father and the smelly man carried the white box with Oliver in it over to where two men were leaning on shovels beside a big pile of fresh earth that smelled very nice. They lowered the box into the ground and threw some freshly cut grass on it and some sod that went thump on the white box. Then the two men filled in the rest of the hole. There were no prayers for small children then and anyway we could not afford a priest, so we just walked back to the carriage with the mother sobbing and looking back over her shoulder. We got in, and the ride home was very short because the horse trotted all the way.

"When we turned the corner into our lane there was a game of soccer going on with all our pals and my father told Frank and myself to run off and play until teatime, and we did, and the boys let us score a lot of goals because our brother had just died."

————

It took me all those years to mentally process Oliver's death and put it down on paper. If death is a mystery to adults, for a child it is impossible to understand. As indiscriminating as it is merciless, death does not care how old you are. Little children suffer through mourning just as much as adults do, and are just as aware of the irretrievable loss, but not why it happened. So when the religious relatives babble to a child that God needs more angels, or when they offer some other sort of the same horseshit, not only are they not helping ease the child's discomfort in dealing with death, they are making it worse by blurring the stark lines that death draws and confusing the child. Thankfully, most children possess a reasonable amount of cynicism that allows them to scramble out from under the avalanches of crap that spew from the mouths of idiots.

I must say, though, I began using the horseshit to my advantage by quietly nominating other kids on the lane to be play pals for the baby Jesus in heaven. There was one bully on the block who I thought should be given a ticket to the clouds as soon as humanly or heavenly possible. I got a whack on the side of the head from my grandma for suggesting it.

———

Nothing is more heartbreaking than the death of a child who has done nothing wrong to man or God except, perhaps, when that death is cheapened by ignorance and myth. The Holy Mother Church of my youth was inundated with both.

# FIVE

# O'Neill's Yank

*A cat in despondency sighed,*
*And resolved to commit suicide.*
*She passed under the wheels of eight automobiles,*
*But under the ninth one she died.*

The adults of the Ireland of my youth were adept at pulling the wool over the eyes of the poor children when it came to death and its aftermath. Can't blame them, though. They knew no better. They experienced the same woolly blindness at the hands of the Catholic Church, the masters of wool pulling. Most of the wool garments in the lanes of Limerick, however, were threadbare enough to see right through.

———

One night, not too long after Oliver's death, I felt Eugene immovably flopped beside me, almost on top of me, and he was icy cold.

"Eugene, please move over," I said. "I can't sleep with you like that."

I pulled my knees up and tried to push him away with them, but he just kept falling back on me.

"Mam, Mam," I yelled. "Eugene won't give me any room."

At least he wasn't coughing and hot with fever as he had been the night before and the night before that.

And of course he was dead, and once more we bravely and solemnly clopped our way back to Saint Patrick's Cemetery to put Eugene's white coffin on top of his brother's container. The father had to restrain the mother from throwing herself into the grave, and she couldn't stay in our previous abode, the single room damp from the river Shannon on Harstonge Street, because everywhere she looked there were all the memories of her small, playful children. Once again the McCourts were on the move, this time into a six-shillings-a-week "two-up two-down" house on Roden Lane, halfway up the steep Barrack Hill.

Roden Lane was a dispirited group of ancient houses wherein existed a largish number of people who came and went. The landlord, Sir Vincent Nash, was one of those absentee Irish traitors whose minions never hesitated to evict the family who couldn't afford the rent that ran about the equivalent of a dollar a week. We were number four Roden Lane, and the communal lavatory was situated just outside our door, which, when opened, would allow in a variety of almost visible stinks from the buckets of shit deposited not very carefully in said lavatory. We called the latrine Bucketham Palace.

Now, much has been written in the body of work produced by various McCourts about the lavatory on Roden Lane, so I won't dig too deeply into the pile of shite it was. But in a book about death, and my views on the ultimate demise, it's important to reiterate the fact that my father, absentee toper as he was, might have been able to save many lives during World War II if only he'd gotten word to Winston Churchill of his plan. That plan consisted of transporting Bawnie Sexton's odiferous bucket to the front, where, with the correct prevailing winds, its stench could wipe out the whole German Army.

What hasn't been covered by the McCourt bookshelf, however, was how yours truly was able to escape the cuckoo clutches of the oppressive Mother Church and its draconian views on sin, heaven, hell, et cetera. As I like to say, organized religion has all the aspects of organized crime except the compassion.

The little ones in Limerick went to the Henry Street School, which was run by nuns. The morn I went is not forgotten. The mother gouged the ear wax out with a rag that she dipped into boiling water, she tightened the patches on my trousers, wiped my snotty nose, and took me by the hand and led me to school. There was an iron gate with spikes that squeaked when you opened it, all very forbidding. A nun was standing on the step at the door, and she was an enormous glowering figure with hard, steely eyes. She wore what looked to me like a hood and a tight white wrap around her face and forehead. I didn't know if she was going to eat me or hit me.

"Leave him here with me," she snapped.

"I don't want to be here," I croaked.

"You shut up."

She grabbed my hand and told the mother to go home. I

had a pair of heavy Saint Vincent de Paul charity boots on, ones that Mam had gotten for my back-to-school outfit. The toe on them was as hard as an iron kettle. As she pulled me with one hand, she used her other to lift her skirt slightly to manage the step. This gave me just a glimpse of a lower leg. I pulled back the booted foot and quickly brought it forward, landing it right on its shiny mark on her shin. She let out a howl and let go of my hand.

By the time I heard the words, "You little blaguard," I was out of the gate and running so hard I beat my mother home.

"And what are you doing here?" she said.

"That old wan was going to eat me," I whined.

My slow departure from the Holy Mother Church continued one day in the lane when I was about seven or eight. A bunch of us were kicking a ball when a new priest approached us.

"Hello, children," he said, and we were astonished that this august presence was talking to us. The priests never did, except in confession or to reprimand. So we gathered around him.

"What's your name?" he said to one of our gang.

"Billy, Fadder," came the answer.

"And what are you going to be when you grow up?"

"I'm going to be an engine driver."

"Ah, that is fine, boy. Fine. And what's your name?" he said to another boy.

"Tommy."

"And Tommy, what are you going to be when you grow up?"

"I'm going to work on the cars, Father, just like my own father."

"Good for you, Tommy."

And then the priest turned to me.

"And your name, son?"

"Junior," I said, as that's what they called me then.

"And what is it that you'll be doing when you're grown, Junior?"

"I'm going to America, Father," I said.

His face turned an angry red.

"What did you say?" he sputtered. "Why would you want to do that?" he thundered. "Don't you know that America is a sinful country? You go there, you'll lose your immortal soul. And if God had meant you to be in America he would have put you there."

"He did, Father," I said in a timid tremble. "I was born there."

You had a better chance of finding the queen's tiara in Limerick than a slum kid who was born in America, and this information stopped him in his tracks. He was flabbergasted. His face looked like a polluted sunset. He stomped away, and as he did, he dragged most of my belief in the Catholic Church with him.

The rest of it went when I discovered masturbation.

Every Saturday the churches of Limerick were packed with lines of people going to confession to scores of celibate priests condemned to listen to the elderly who had eaten a sausage on Friday and little boys who played with their own wieners any chance they got.

After I discovered the joys of masturbation, I couldn't keep my hands off myself. I had made a habit of going to an old foreign priest who wasn't hard on me: a couple of Hail Marys and keep your hands out of your pockets was my usual atonement.

But one Saturday I popped into the confessional and my foreign man was absent and had been replaced by one who seemed like a young, sharp laddie and who tut-tutted as I sputtered my tale of the sins of the flesh. *Impure acts* was the official term for my sins, but unofficially we called it wanking or pulling the pud or, my favorite, shaking hands with the unemployed. The new priest seemed to be appalled at the extent of my self-abuse and asked a question that hung in the air:

"Did you take pleasure in it?"

At first I thought it was a trick question. Once before, confessing the same sin to my regular priest, I had been asked if I'd lost my substance. I promised to tell him the following week after I'd visited the dictionary to find out what the hell he was talking about. But this time I realized that if I told this priest I'd taken pleasure, my sin would be doubled at least. On the other hand (so to speak), if I said I hadn't, I'd feel like a bloody eejit.

Hoping to keep the sins to a minimum, I gave the correct if untrue answer and thought I was off the hook and would've been had my foreigner heard my confession. Instead a swift intake of breath on the other side of the screen came, followed by an exhalation of dreadful news. The God man launched into a diatribe that terrified me. He told me that every time I used myself in an impure manner I was driving another nail into the hands of Jesus and poking him with the spear in his wounded side and causing him suffering that was inconceivable. I didn't know why he was picking on me, because we didn't even own a hammer and didn't have a use for nails, and I certainly never saw a crucifixion in Limerick. But that didn't stop him, and because of all the suffering I was causing

Jesus by continuing my impure practices, he could not see any point in giving me absolution for my sins. I would have to come to him the following week, he said. And not in the confessional but face-to-face at the priest's residence.

In broad daylight?

Not shrouded by the confessional screen?

The horror of it! He would certainly know who I was! And if that wasn't terrifying enough, he told me that I had to stay pure in thought, word, and deed. Four whole days of hands off! Why not just have me saw the willy off and bury it somewhere where a dog might dig it up? If I didn't follow his directions, he said, it was straight to hell for me.

And the hell he described was merciless. In this hell the devil concentrated on the part of the body that had committed the sin. If you've been looking at dirty pictures, then the devil sticks hot pokers in your eyes. If you've put your hands where they shouldn't be, he chops them off, after which they grow back to be chopped off again. If the legs are involved in lewd dancing, he burns them down to the hips over and over. The ears that heard dirty stories are filled by funnels of molten lead. The tongue that tells lurid stories is lanced and split by a red-hot razor. The worst torture perhaps was saved for the pee-pee and testies. Over a cauldron of boiling steel you were dangled horizontally, and the wee apparatuses were dipped into the liquefied fire again and again for all of eternity. As severe as the penalties were, the thought that kept infiltrating the mind was that my wanking might be worth it. This all reminds me of the old joke of the dad who tells the son that if he keeps masturbating, he'll go blind.

"Can I do it until I need glasses?" the son asks.

I tried to clear my mind, which was leaping about from ecstasy to the eternity of hell, by making my way to the Lyric Cinema for the twopenny matinee, a fillum as we called it. I arrived, however, five minutes after the fillum had started, and the policy of the movie house was that latecomers were charged double the price, or fourpence. I knew that God was punishing me for my sins, as fourpence was far beyond my financial reach at the time, and no doubt he knew that I'd watched *Tarzan the Ape Man* four times in the hope of Jane's torn toggery riding up enough for a look at the promised land. Interestingly, perhaps, years later I would become friendly with Maureen O'Sullivan, who played Jane in the early Tarzan flicks. A delight, she laughed when I told her of my boyhood fascination.

"I'm happy I was tastily dressed," she said.

Back at the Lyric Cinema, there was no doubt in my mind that God was watching me and that he was very pissed off about the number of nails I'd hammered into his son's hands. I thought that maybe he would drop an airplane right out of the sky and onto my cranium, this thought arriving even though it was wartime and there were very few passenger planes flying over Limerick. Still, I didn't know whether to walk close to the buildings or far away from them. I didn't want my sins to kill any innocent home dwellers, because they certainly didn't do anything wrong or have impure thoughts that I knew of, and I wasn't sure how good God's aim was. Horses were plentiful on the streets in those days, and frightened runaway horses were not uncommon, and so that was dangerous too. I knew God would tell them to aim for me. There was a severe shortage of petrol, and the few cars were powered by odd peat-burning contraptions locked on the rear end, but slow as they were I was taking no chances of being run over.

At night I was afraid to go to sleep, as there were stories of people going to sleep and not waking up, just like Eugene. Had I remembered the Church's teaching on contrition I would not have suffered the prepangs of hell. Holy Mother Church says there are two forms of contrition, the first of which is imperfect contrition, to wit: *Listen, God, I am sorry to have done all those rotten things as I'm really terrified of going to hell and having my pee-pee dipped in molten steel for all eternity; just the thought of it gives me the shivers, so I hope you can bring your famous amnesia to bear on all the things I've done that piss you off.*

Perfect contrition goes something like this: *Listen, God, I'm awfully sorry I sinned, because you are such a terrific, merciful, compassionate, and open-minded good sport, and the sorts of things I've done are very distasteful and an affront to the wonderfulness of you. I'm sorry, and what I did to Jesus is unfortunate.*

Now, under these tenets the Church would gladly have forgiven even Hitler, who was born a Catholic, by the way, had he adhered to the latter type of contrition above, e.g., *Sorry, God, for all the damage, but I know you see the good in me because you made me, after all, so I was hoping to join you, Mary, Joseph, and the kid in the heavenly abode for the rest of ever and I hope you still have the house policy of excluding Jews, homos, cripples, and the mentally ill. Heil Hitler!* There are Christians who pray like that.

After four terror-filled days, I found myself alone at 3:00

p.m. on Wednesday ringing the priest's bell. I was ushered into an unfriendly parlor with grim framed faces looking down from the wall at me as if they knew my transgressions. The young, hip father met me there wearing a quizzical expression.

"What can I do for you?" he asked.

"You told me to come for absolution."

"I did? Why?"

"I dunno, Fadder."

I wanted to scream, "What about the pokers? The molten lead? The boiling steel into which my pee-pee would be dipped?"

"Kneel," he said grimly, pointing to the threadbare carpet. I did as he told me.

"Now say a sincere act of contrition."

"O my God, I am heartily sorry for having offended you…"

"Off you go," the father said when I was done, and I didn't care if all of Limerick collapsed and planes fell out of the sky and every horse reared and galloped right toward me. I was in that beautiful place called "the state of grace," for which every devout Catholic yearns. For now, if I was hit by a falling building or plane, or mowed down by a car or horse, I'd be going straight to heaven and would be happy at the right hand of God for all eternity.

Of course, there was the usual uprising in the fly department ever demanding to be relieved, to be quickly followed by the thought of hammering another nail into the foot or hand of Jesus popping into the cranium! But I couldn't have been the only one. There must have been guys like me all over the world doing it. How many nails could fit into one pair of palms and one pair of feet? And if heaven was a place of eternal happiness, why did the God Guy allow his only begotten son to keep getting hammered?

The thought of either sitting at the right hand of God or using my right hand to pleasure myself kept me up at night. Was heaven filled with happy people who had stopped pulling the pud?

For a twelve-year-old, it wasn't a fair fight. The hell with the church, I said; once more my mind wandered to Mrs. Tarzan in her skimpy rear covering. I began to lose myself in thoughts about Jane in her togs.

———————

What Frank, Mike, Alphie, and I learned from growing up in Limerick can't be taught in any school or university on this earth. The art of storytelling was endemic to the city, and the love of songs and music was as natural to Limerick people as breathing to everyone else. I don't remember ever learning songs, but we knew dozens of them as though they were planted somehow in our brains as we slept. And so, it seemed, did everyone else in Limerick.

There was a man named Paddy Reidy who sold newspapers and was very proud of his operatic voice. In Limerick people admired things foreign as long as they didn't move in. You'd hear Reidy's wavering tenor: "Come back again, beloved / Back to Sorrento, / Or I must die and buy the *Limerick Leader*." Paddy adored the opera. One time, it was said, he wrote a fan letter to Beniamino Gigli, the great Italian tenor of his generation. Reidy, however, was fluent only in Italian song and not on the page, so he did the best he could in a sort of pidgin, phonetic Italian. Gigli got the greatest kick out of Paddy's letter and wrote back. Then, not too long after, the tenor happened to be giving a concert in Dublin and sent a chauffeured limousine to Limerick to pick up Paddy Reidy. From that moment on you could hear the newspaper seller all the way across the Shannon singing, "*La donna è mobile, / Qual piuma al vento, / Muta d'accento, e di pensiero.*" You never knew what could happen when you sang a song in Limerick.

Then there were our next-door neighbors, Mary and Sean Costelloe, who were two of the best tellers of tales. Sean was a salesman, and most of his customers had no money and would buy his wares on what he called "the Kathleen Mavourneen plan." "Kathleen Mavourneen" was an old song, popularized in Ireland by the soprano Catherine Hayes, that contained the line "It may be for years, and it may be forever."

———

Although the education by osmosis enriched us, a more traditional type of learning was foisted onto us at Leamy's National School, better known as the Leamy Academy of Surgeons because the masters there were known to draw blood when they whacked us. Our teachers carried an assortment of gear that would make Caligula blush. They had leather straps, canes, ash plants, and blackthorn sticks with knobs for beating pupils for every possible crime and misdemeanor. The worst of the punishments, though, was something called "pinching."

This particular S&M technique involved the teacher trying to lift you up by your sideburns until tears flowed from your eyes like two small trout streams.

There was Dotty O'Neill, called that because he was small as a dot. He would make us cut a switch from a tree and then whip us with it. There was Tasher Scanlon, called that because of the mustache he wore, and Mad Gilligan, who had the worst temper of all.

And then there was Puddledy O'Dea, who tortured us with the catechism and told us how the English murdered the Irish for eight hundred years. One day Puddledy asked Frank why God made the world, and the brother said, "To have something to stand on."

I didn't do well in school. But I can't put all the blame on the teachers. I was blocked in learning grammar and mathematics. My attention span was minuscule. Today I would be diagnosed with some learning disability, but back then you were just a daydreamer. The master talked about verbs and adjectives, and I'd find myself gazing out the window. I thought a dangling participle had something to do with sex. They also taught the Irish language. Gaelic grammar is as complicated as German; it's a tough language to learn, and I was lost at sea.

So when the time came for the test for the primary school certificate, I didn't have much of a chance to pass, and I didn't.

I don't know how much not having graduated primary school, or grammar school as it's called in the US, mattered in my life. I suppose it added another brick to the load of shame I carried. But it certainly didn't keep me from advancing out of

Limerick, and, after all, that was the whole point of going to school in the first place—to get out of the slum.

Many years later, after I'd written and published *A Monk Swimming*, I, along with the brothers, was invited to Washington to lend support for Project Children. Started by an NYPD bomb squad cop named Denis Mulcahy, the organization brought Catholic and Protestant children from the North of Ireland to America, where one of each would spend summers with a host family. It was a way to build a bridge of friendship between the two sides during the Troubles and a way to find that perceived enemies did not have horns, tails, and cloven hoofs.

The Irish minister of education happened to be at the affair we attended. He struck up a conversation with me.

"Where did you get your degree?" he asked.

"What degree?"

"University?"

"Don't have one."

"Whatchu mean?"

"Never went."

"Well, where'd you go to secondary school?"

"Never went."

"Why not?"

"Didn't graduate from primary school."

"You've had books published and on the *New York Times* best-seller list?"

"Correct."

"And you didn't get the primary?"

"Also correct."

"How did you do that?"

"Well, I read a lot and just rearranged the words and wrote them down." That amused the man.

Several weeks later I received a call from the Irish ambassador. He was calling at the behest of the minister, and said that the Irish Department of Education and Science was going to do something that had never been done. It was going to award me an honorary primary school certificate. I proudly hung it in the hallway of my apartment.

When I was about fourteen, and without a diploma, I joined the Irish Army to be a band trainee. I was supposed to learn the theories of music and master the trumpet, and was useless and hopeless in both departments. The brother Frank was a terrific drummer. He could throw the drumsticks up in the air and behind his back and catch them without missing a beat. I, on the other hand, couldn't carry a tune in a wheelbarrow, never mind on a trumpet. What made my time there even more uncomfortable was that the regular soldier bandsmen were preying on all of us young boys. It was a battle just to fend them off.

One day the top sergeant summoned me to the orderly room, where he informed me that my maternal grandmother was in the hospital and was close to death. He gave me compassionate leave to go to Limerick. So I got my train pass, and because I didn't have civilian clothing I just packed the uniform stuff and off I went to the hometown. I stepped down from the train and boarded a bus for the City Home, as they called the hospital. The various wards had about twenty-four beds each, twelve on either side, and Grandma Sheehan was four beds down on the left side. There was that angry face, flushed, and the white hair with the mouth drooping open and breathing the long, loud gasps that Frank and I called "the Sheehans' chest." It didn't matter if a Sheehan was on death's door or suffering just from the sniffles, the sound they emanated was the same, a hacking *hah, hah, hah*. Standing there and listening to Grandma, I thought of Frank and stifled a laugh. But then the hacking stopped, and she was dead.

The nurse came in and confirmed it. The hospital worker prepared the body, placed it in a coffin, and brought it to the church, where it stayed overnight, which was customary at the time. Meanwhile the neighbors dug the grave in Mungret Cemetery in the Sheehan plot. There were no full-time gravediggers, at least for the poor of Limerick.

The neighbors also shouldered the coffin into the horse-drawn hearse, and off it went on Grandma's last ride. I stood in my army band uniform and watched as they lowered her into the earth. If I'd had my trumpet I would have played something off-key.

---

After failing as a musician, I found my way to Whatstandwell, Derbyshire, where I worked as a houseboy at a Benedictine school. I had to make the beds, serve meals, and clean the toilets. In charge was a housekeeper who was an elegant, well-spoken Englishwoman in her forties. She could have easily played a role on *Downton Abbey*. I knew that she liked classical music and one day, to have her believe I was a bright, well-informed fellow, I let it drop that I had been listening to the Polish pianist Paderewski on the radio the night before. I think she was impressed that I even knew the name, never mind the man's music. She invited me to an opera in Covent Garden. The opera was *Il trovatore*. I thought it was grand, but one critic disagreed. He said it was the tenor who made Trovatore ill.

———

From Whatstandwell I went to Coventry, where I worked in the various factories, the first of which was Courtaulds, a manufacturer of fabric and clothing. From Courtaulds I went to Dunlop, where I made bicycle wheels. From Dunlop I got a job in the gasworks, where I was a stoker and shoveled coal into a furnace all night like O'Neill's Yank in *The Hairy Ape*. It was 1947, and soldiers were back from the war and jobs not easy to get. I was only sixteen, and I shouldn't have been working there anyhow, so I was lucky to have the job even though I was skinny as a waif and had to shovel coal all night into a furnace that was like the gates of hell.

I slept in a boardinghouse on Cope Street with twenty-four cuckoo, hard-drinking Irish lunatics. I wasn't drinking at the time at all. I'd joined up with the local Scouts, and that kept me on the straight. I had a small bed next to the window in a room on the third floor with three of the imbibing Micks, who slept across two beds pushed together. One of them staggered in every Friday night, legless from the drink, bellowing as he opened the window.

"That's it for me," he'd wail, "I'm going to jump."

We were on the third floor. We'd all have to get out of bed and stop him from jumping and calm him down. One Friday night in he comes and launches into his routine, but this night, it being two in the morning, I'm dead tired, and I can't even raise my head. The other guys must have been out of it because all of a sudden there's no commotion or bellowing, just silence. I open my eyes and he's not there. I get up and look out the window and there he is down in the courtyard and the moon is shining on him naked as can be, his white body outlined against the cobblestones, still as death.

"It wasn't the jump that got him," one of the lads said. "It was the sudden stop."

We thought he was dead. He wasn't. He'd broken a hip, and lived to jump another day.

Peter Grant was one of the lunatics who resided in the boardinghouse with me. He worked full-time at Jaguar and part-time at a butcher, primarily because he was able to take scraps and odd pieces of meat home. A tiny couple named Gaughin kept the boardinghouse.

"I have something special for you and the other young lad," Mrs. G whispered one night to me at dinner. "So don't eat too much. I'll give it to you after everyone's finished."

She served the plates to us after everyone had left.

"Rabbit," she said. "Delicious."

The other lad and I scarfed down the meal, and after we had finished Peter Grant came into the kitchen.

"How'd you enjoy your rabbit, boys? Here's the rest of him," he said as he threw a catskin on the table.

He was just a mean-spirited arsehole, and I never ate another rabbit or looked at a cat the same way again.

————————

My boss at the gasworks was a Scot. A burly man, he had slightly graying hair, a twinkle in his eye, and a good sense of humor. He was also communist and more of a Marxist than a Stalinist, Stalin being your typical everyday dictator. We would have talks while the furnace burned in front of us.

A member of the union, he was a very decent, principled working-class guy. I was struck by how similar his Marxist views were to the ideas in the papal encyclicals of Pope Leo XIII and Pius XI that I had read. Justice for the workingman was the theme in both cases. I asked him about religion and God and he was fascinated by both my questions and my ignorance.

He was the first person to tell me about the Vatican's department of propaganda, *Propaganda Fide*, and how propaganda is advertising at its root and not strictly used to spread falsehoods, as is commonly believed. He said that the Catholic Church wanted Catholics to have more children, or "recruits," he called them. Though Marxists don't believe in God, and Marx himself said that religion is the opiate of the people, the Scot wasn't a militant opponent of the Church. He was more a man of the moment, Buddhist, almost, in a way. Maybe it was the open fire in front of us, one that reminded me of the hell that the Church had promised me for offenses as ridiculous as impure thoughts, that got me thinking. But the Scot and his soliloquies had a profound effect on me and would begin to shape my beliefs in what an afterlife might hold.

Leamy's was a secular school, but a secular school as one could be only in Ireland, which meant the parish priest oversaw it. So we did have religious instruction in the way of catechism in prep for First Communion. It was taught in a savage way that drove many of us out of the Church and into the arenas of cynicism, agnosticism, and atheism. But it also led me to have a look at other faiths and other beliefs with a mixture of curiosity and skepticism. I read books on Zionism and the beginnings of Israel, read the Koran, and, later, got the arse to India and looked closely at Hinduism and dove into Buddhism.

I bolstered my conversations with the Scot with my nascent knowledge of religion. Unlike O'Neill's Yank, I felt no fulfillment through the labor I performed in the gasworks. But in front of the furnace I began to forge a belief in myself and not in some mystical being. Even the small, childlike part of me that held on to hope that there might be a heaven began to disappear. And the furnace I fed was as close as I was going to get to the hell the Church had warned me about.

———

I was like Yank in one respect, though. I would soon be on an ocean liner heading for America.

———

When I was eighteen, I went back to Limerick for a holiday and decided to stay, for what reason I do not know. Frank, who was in Limerick the whole time I was away, had sailed to America. He had been working for a magazine distributor called Eason's in Limerick. Working in the office. An inside job. Left that for America.

When I came home, I moved in with my uncle, Ab Sheehan. Ab delivered the *Limerick Leader* and was a few issues short of a bundle. We used to say that he'd been dropped on his head when he was a baby. My father was off to England, and the mother, Angela, was still living with Laman Griffin, whom I hated. After the father left, we were evicted from our slum dwelling and lived in another small house with one tiny room and with a little loft. Along with the brothers, I lived there under Laman's drunken thumb for four years, from ten to fourteen. He was extremely nasty and hit us for no reason. Belted us. He worked as a lineman for the ESB, the Electrical Supply Board, and they called him "Laman" because his mother sold toffee apples, which were called lamans. At least that's the story I heard. He had been a good rugby player in his day and played for a team of high repute in Limerick called Young Munster. He was an only child and his mother's pet.

On Friday nights he'd come home with a piece of steak and tell Angela to cook it. We had nothing. The pleasant aroma of the frying beef filled the house, but he would sit there and eat it all by himself, except for the bits of fat and bone that he'd feed to Lucky, our dog. The dog was lucky.

He would then summon the mother to his upstairs lair, where he made no attempt to muffle the groaning and grunting of their drunken fucking. My brother Frank wrote about this stuff in *Angela's Ashes*, and it was the only part of the book that caused him to hesitate. When the book came out the reaction, from Limerick especially, was one of shock and outrage. I told him if he hadn't included the scene we both remembered clearly, the essence of his book would be illusionary and puzzling. It happened and needed to be told to support our experience. That's why I'm telling it again.

We knew it was wrong what they were doing. We knew Laman shouldn't be eating meat on Friday too. We used to pray that he'd fall off a pole and break his neck. At one point I decided I would kill him. Beat him to death with a hurling stick. The plan went only as far as the thinking stage. But I did think about it.

I thought about it a lot.

Even when I returned to Limerick, the thought sizzled in the back of the mind like the steak Angela cooked for him.

I got a job in a motor works in the parts department. I didn't like the job. Too dangerous. A truck rolled over my foot in the garage. The X-ray didn't show a break, but it was painful to stand, which I did at a window all day long, and that was after having to walk a mile to work. Still, they insisted I come in. I was supposed to write all the parts I gave to the mechanics in a book, but one day I forgot and they fired me.

After I was fired from the motor works I took a job as a houseboy at the Jesuits' residence, where I polished their shoes and floors and cleaned their toilets. From the Jesuits, a friend named Seán South got me a job at McMahon's timber yard. I measured the timber coming off the ships.

At the time I was nineteen and measuring planks, with no money to speak of, living with my mentally challenged uncle and with no girlfriend. There was no occasion for sin, no dirty movies or dirty magazines; I had just my imagination. Which was limited too.

If I'd stayed in Limerick, I don't know what would have happened. Probably I'd have ended up as one of the corner boys, the guys with the greasy hair smoking Woodbine fags.

Meanwhile, the brother Frank was working at the Biltmore Hotel in midtown Manhattan, where he was charged with the care of sixty caged canaries in the public room. Thirty-nine of them died of neglect; after that the brother taped the lifeless bodies to their perches. This canary holocaust was discovered when Frank took off for Saint Patrick's Day and didn't show up at work until two days later.

My brother, the bird murderer, paid for my steamer ticket.

When I walked up our little hill, I turned and looked back for the last time.

And I was off on the good ship *America* to the land of my birth in my dead uncle's suit. Sixteen years earlier I had sailed with the other McCourts, hoping to leave the death of Margaret Mary behind, only to watch the twins, my friends, and Pa Keating die in Limerick.

I wanted to go where they knew how to live.

# SIX

# The Raincoat Brigade

*"I hadn't the heart to touch my breakfast.*
*I told Jeeves to drink it himself."*

P. G. WODEHOUSE,

*MY MAN JEEVES*

In 1952 I sailed back across the Atlantic on a ship named for my destination, America. Dead Pa Keating's suit hung heavy on my frame and was incongruous as I sat by the onboard swimming pool. It had been eighteen years since the smiling little fellow, so charming and cunning, had sailed in the other direction. I didn't know what lay ahead, only what I was leaving behind.

On the ship I met a couple named Harrington who worked for the City of New York. Mrs. H was a dietitian of some sort and ran the food services for the hospitals and nurses' residence on Welfare Island, now known as Roosevelt Island. She arranged a job for me. When I showed up the first day, they handed me a spotless white jacket and white pants. For a fleeting moment I thought they were going to give me a scalpel.

Instead they led me to the kitchen in the nurses' residence, where they gave me a pair of rubber gloves and a sponge.

Along with hospitals and nurses, Welfare Island was also the home of a young women's detention center. The inmates there were called PINs, persons in need. I worked my dish-washing job from seven in the morning to two in the afternoon and would have to stroll by the jailhouse on my way to the Fifty-Ninth Street Bridge and my walk home. As I passed the jail, the young female inmates would yell at me to do things with them that I'd never heard about in my life, let alone experienced, as I was still shaking hands with the unemployed at the time.

I lived in a small furnished room on Third Avenue and Fifty-Eighth Street. The apartment had a gas stove, and the bathroom was down the hall. The rent was nine dollars a week, nine times what it was for a slum house in Limerick.

At the time, brother Frank was in Germany in the US Army. So I was pretty much on my own here in America. But not for long. I received a very nice letter from the US Selective Service System inviting me into the army. I knew enough to know I didn't want to go to Korea, which was raging at the time, so I hied myself down to the United States Air Force recruitment center and joined the air force before the army joined me.

My military career was uneventful except for one ringing exception. The air force sent me to a hospital base in England, and there I met the woman who led me down the path of the sins of the flesh. She was a captain in the nursing corps of the US Air Force, and very accomplished in the bedroom business. On leave she'd whisk me off to London for short stays where we saw little more than the inside of a hotel room. Years of pent-up sexual ignorance, heightened by the visions at the Lyric Cinema such as Maureen O'Sullivan's revealing drapery, cascaded and sang, and bands played and lovers professed, and I was a man, at last, in every possible description of the term.

It was almost certainly worth the wait.

I don't know how much relevance virginity and the loss thereof have in a book on death, except perhaps the inevitable parallel of passing of innocence. With the male of our species, virginity is strictly a state of mind without any physical changes. Young lads are prone to fabricating sexual conquests because they think having intercourse makes them more manly, and although the advent of sex is part of the maturation process, becoming a man has more to do with character than where you put your pee-pee. For both men and women, the importance of virginity exists in the mind more than in any part of the body. In fact, it's a question of semantics if you ask me. I think of the radical terrorists who believe that for blowing themselves up they will receive a significant number of virgins in heaven. The Koran documents this reward, they say. Unfortunately for the suicide bomber, much can get lost in translation. For instance, in Syrian, the Arabic word for virgin means raisins, white raisins to be exact. So what happens if the Syrian translation is the correct word of the Prophet Muhammad? Then you blow yourself to smithereens, and someone hands you a bowl containing seventy-two raisins and tells you to go sate yourself?

Even if the Arabic translation is the correct word, things can go haywire. The process happens as such: These laddies strap explosives around the waist, go out and press a button, and off the body goes, the head, the legs, the arms, the fingers, the cock, followed by the testicles, the heart, the kidneys, the liver, and bone dust all blown all the way to paradise, where God's mechanics are kept busy reassembling the pieces. Then you're presented with seventy-two virgins and the instructions to mount all of them. Here you are, just having gotten yourself together after a long and arduous journey, and you're not even given the chance to have a ham sandwich or a glass of milk, let alone the opportunity to get used to the new equipment. And what happens if the assemblers mislay your penis?

Though seventy-two might seem to you like an enormous number, the amount apparently isn't so large when you're a reattached young man in his twenties. But then what? Are the virgins restored to factory condition? Or are they disposed of because, after all, they're only women?

As I am eighty-four and far too far along on my journey to go into hiding like Salman Rushdie or find myself as a headliner in some beheading video, I don't want you to think I'm judging these beliefs. So if you believe you're going to screw your reattached arse off in paradise, blow yourself away at will. But do everybody a favor, pull the pin, or press the button, in your own lavatory. If you do, there'll be shithouse explosions from here to East Jabib. Fox News once reported that the Iraqis alone had hundreds of seasoned suicide bombers.

———————

I was twenty-three when the air force discharged me, and life, not death, beckoned, although it wasn't exactly a glamorous existence at first. I moved across the Hudson River from Fifty-Eighth Street in Manhattan to Jersey City and took a job as a concrete inspector for the New Jersey Turnpike. Yes, there is such a position. I worked in a place called a batching plant, where I judged how much cement to mix in with the sand and crushed stone. I had to be vigilant. The moment I turned my back, someone would bollix up the process and water the mixture. Heavily watered concrete is dangerous when you're traveling seventy miles an hour—it's not a motorboat you're propelling. So I consider myself something of a hero, as the lives I probably saved are countless.

I worked at the plant for two and a half years. They paid me $300 once a month. My room and board at the time was $150, so I had a bit of disposable income, which I disposed of quickly. Too quickly. After I was there a year or so I asked for a raise. They gave you a form to fill out that had a space where you explained the reason for your request. "There's too much month left at the end of my money," I wrote. I got a twenty-dollar bump in the pay.

Most of my free time and money were spent across the Hudson River. The New York City of the early to mid-1950s was a glorious place. In his lovely 1949 essay called *Here Is New York*, E. B. White sums up the energy of the marvelous metropolis like this: "Commuters give the city its tidal restlessness; natives give it solidity and continuity; but the settlers give it passion." Although I was living in New Jersey at the time, I carried my eagerness into New York each weekend, where I savored the delights of Manhattan. As P. G. Wodehouse once wrote, "What's the use of a great city having temptations if fellows don't yield to them?"

I wasn't exactly climbing the corporate ladder, but I did make a career move by taking a job as a longshoreman. I worked the New York Harbor waterfront on both the Jersey and Manhattan sides; only the Brooklyn docks were verboten, for Red Hook was the province of the Italians, who would say to me in no uncertain terms, "No Micks allowed here."

After some time in Jersey, I became weary of the PATH commute under the river and took an apartment with two roommates on the Upper West Side. The rental was across the street from the Museum of Natural History, one of the great depositories of human knowledge, but it didn't, to my knowledge, have a liquor license, so I didn't step foot in the place.

Frank too, long back from the army, was working the docks around this time and assorted other odd jobs, including in a bank at night. He was also taking classes at NYU, readying himself for a career in front of the classroom. In 1956 Frank was living in a cold-water flat in Greenwich Village that, for reasons never adequately explained, had plenty of hot water. After a few months with the lads uptown, I gathered my worldly belongings, which fit neatly into one small suitcase, and rattled my way via subway to the bowels of Manhattan.

It was while living with Frank that I came up with a nearly brilliant idea to assuage the inconvenience of the monthly bills. I went to a local stationery store, where I bought a rubber stamp that read "deceased" and a pad of red ink. When the Con Ed bill arrived, I stamped it with the notification and sent the envelope back to the company. Frank and I then lived on a free feed from the electric provider until the lights went out a couple of months later. The moral of the story is that when it comes to finances, the pretense of death is a short-term fix. Only the real thing solves your money problems in the long run.

It was during these years, as you might have surmised, that my alcohol consumption began to gain steam, and with the intake, an outward personality began to form. In a way this wasn't a bad thing. I carried so much shame from the poverty of my childhood that absent the booze I might have been frozen in fear. Instead I drank so I wouldn't feel the fear, and turned the shame into a sort of false bravado that formed a shield. Absent the fear and shame I was impenetrable, and with a personality that filled all the space around me.

I spent the summer of 1956 in a share house on Fire Island and took a job selling Bibles to the beach community for a little extra cash. *Little* is the operative word in that sentence. If you ask me how many Bibles I sold that summer, I could give you the exact number: none. But my walking on the beach in my bathing suit, a drink in one hand and a Bible in the other, drew the attention and admiration of the bathers lounging on the sand.

Of the people I became friendly with on Fire Island was a cadre of amusing lads including Pat McCormick, who was then in the beginnings of a celebrated career as a comedy writer and comic actor, and Tom O'Malley, a comedy writer and a booker for *Tonight,* the early version of *The Tonight Show,* then starring Jack Paar.

At summer's end, and back in the gray caverns of New York, the party continued. I became a habitué of a joint called Clavin's on Manhattan's East Side. The bartender there was a P. G. Wodehouse fan, and we immediately hit it off. In the back of the shoebox of a bar was a piano behind which, on alternate nights, sat the brother of the then Broadway star Shirley MacLaine. Warren Beatty, of course, would go on to garner a bit of his own spotlight. The other tinkler of the ivory keys was a fellow named Peter Duchin, son of a famous orchestra leader, and he too would find a following of his own. There was a third piano player named Buddy Lewis, whose father was Fulton Lewis, the Rush Limbaugh of his day.

Now, it wasn't as if I were in the bars every night. On the third Thursday of every other month, I took in the theater so as not to let the cultured part of my brain dry up like a discarded olive. As it happened, conveniently situated around the corner from Clavin's was the Theatre East on Sixtieth Street near Second Avenue. One Thursday night I wandered in to watch three one-acts by the playwright John Millington Synge, and my life changed. Never before had I heard the English language soar to such heights. John Millington Synge said that words should have the texture of a crisp autumn apple. I was enraptured by the writing and bitten by the theater bug all at once. On the sidewalk, after the play, a thought descended on me like a brick falling from the buildings above.

"This is where I belong," I said to myself.

My whole life, my miserable childhood, my discussions

with the communist in front of the furnace, the watering of the cement, had all led me to this point: I was meant to tread the boards!

I turned on my heels and marched back into the theater and demanded an audience with the boss.

"You mean the producer?" came the response.

"Indeed!"

"I'm him," says he.

"I want to be part of your group," says I.

"And what kind of acting experience do you have?"

"I'm Irish," says I.

"Say no more."

I was hired on the spot. I didn't have a headshot, a résumé, or any of the other things germane to the profession. They used my passport photo for the theater program. It was also at this time that my two worlds melded into one. After rehearsal I led the players and audience like a pie-eyed piper around the corner to Clavin's. There we would discuss acting technique, such as it was, and solve the rest of the world's problems. I thought the theater crowd brought some needed color to the joint. The proprietor of the saloon thought otherwise. One night Clavin himself pulled me to the side.

"If you plan to keep bringing in these actor types you better get behind the bar and serve them," he said. "Because I'm not going to anymore."

And so, simultaneously, my career as an actor and my career as a barman began. There are similarities between the two paths. The actor and the bartender are both performers, dispensing joy, comfort, and escape to all who enter their respective arenas. The occupations also go together like whiskey and soda.

In a short time I landed a part in an off-Broadway play and was on local late-night television promoting such, and working a very busy bar and drinking nearly as much as I served, except my customers were buying the stuff and I wasn't. Oh, what a great country is America!

One night I was behind the bar at Clavin's when the phone rang. Tom O'Malley, the lad I'd met on Fire Island, was on the line. It seemed that O'Malley was trolling the deep waters of Manhattan's saloons for guests for *Tonight*. Things were done that way back then.

"It's three hundred bucks for the gig," he says to me.

"I'll be there with bells on," says I.

Actually, I wore a kilt. They booked me for New Year's Day night, which, as everyone knows, is Hogmanay, the Scottish holiday. Appropriately garbed in the Scottish tradition, I went commando to several parties that day on the East Side of Manhattan. Surprisingly, few understood the significance of my outfit. In fact, the only thing Scottish about the affairs I attended was the whiskey being served and drunk.

The last stop was at O'Malley's apartment, which was brimming with mirth and booze. Dressed in a white sheet as Baby New Year, Pat McCormick lobbied to lower the legal drinking age to one. Though I owned what is commonly known in drinking circles as a hollow leg, I was not entirely immune to the effects of the alcohol. I found myself in such an intoxicated state that choosing the correct word to describe the condition I was in is something of a chore. Here are a few of the choices I came up with:

Addled battered beery befuddled befuggered bent besotted bevvied up bibacious bibulous blacked out bladdered blasted blathered bleezin blitzed blootered blotto boiled bombed boogaloo boozed up boozy bosko buckled buttered buttoned buzzed cabbaged canned Chevy Chased clobbered cockeyed corned crapulous crocked dead to the world decimated dipso drunk fecked feeling no pain fleemered floothered flushed four to the floor fried fuddled full as a goog full of loudmouth soup gassed gutted giddy goosed groggy gubbed guttered half-crocked half in the bag hammered having a jag on having the whirlygigs high higher than a kite hooched up hosed housed howling in a stupor inebriated in my cups intemperate intoxicated juiced kippered lamped langered legless liquored up liquorish lit lit like a Christmas tree lit up loaded locked looped lubricated lushy lush mangled mashed maudlin mellow Merle Haggarded merry minced monged monkey-faced mottled Moulin Rouged muddled muzzy Newcastled obfuscated obliterated obliviated oblonctorated off my face off my pickle off my trolley off the wagon on a bender on a spree on the turps out cold out of control out of it out of my tree over the limit on laughing syrup paggered paralytic paralyzed peelywally peevied phalanxed pickled pie-eyed pished pissed piss-eyed pixilated plastered plotzed plowed poleaxed pollatic polluted potted potulent primed rat-arsed rat-legged ratted ravaged razzled red ripped rip-roaring roaring rubbered ruined sauced schlitzed schnockered schnooked screwed scuppered scuttered seeing double shickered shitfaced shithoused slagged slaughtered slizzard slopped up sloppy sloshed slozzled smashed snockered sodden soused sizzled spaced spangled spiffed spifflicated splashed splattered squiffy squished steampigged stewed stiff stinking stinko stoned swacked tanked three sheets to the wind tiddly tight tipsy toasted totaled transmogrified trashed trousered tweaked twisted twizzled under the influence under the table under the weather unsober unsteady vulcanized warped wasted wee lubricated whaled Williamed Winehoused wiped out wired with the fairies woofled woozy wrecked zombied zoned and zonked

So pick two or three of the above, and you'll have a pretty good idea of how drunk I was when O'Malley whisked me off to Jack Paar's talker.

Here's what I remember from that night: I'm still in my kilt. Blinding lights. Riotous laughter. Loud applause. And the Jack Paar guy asking me to come back, which I did some twenty times.

Apparently, Malachy McCourt was a hit.

Death be damned. There was life to live.

———

I would like to interrupt the proceedings by telling an old joke, the one about Hannity, who was killed in an accident on the job. O'Reilly, his coworker, was instructed to go and inform Hannity's wife.

"Break the news gently," the foreman told O'Reilly.

O'Reilly knocked on the door, which was answered by a woman.

"Are you the widow Hannity?" he asked.

Some wise man, maybe Confucius, once said, "If you choose a job you love you will never have to work a day in your life." I was never a fan of the four-letter word for employment, and from the moment I began to act and tend bar I did all I could to sidestep the inconvenience of a job. I didn't set out to follow the Chinese lad's advice, it just sort of followed me.

One night at Clavin's, not too long after one of my *Tonight* appearances, two fellows asked if I would be interested in going into the bar business with them.

"I might be interested in buying a Picasso painting," I told them. "But I barely have the money to buy the *New York Post* newspaper."

"We don't want your money," they said. "All we want is your personality."

"And in return?" I asked.

"Fifteen percent and your name on the awning."

"Hold on," I said. "I'll run it by my attorney."

I turned and looked at my reflection in the mirror behind

the bar. The image was a shock of red hair the size of an eagle's nest, and red beard to match. God, what a handsome lad, I thought.

"I'm in," I said, back on the line.

---

We found an available bar on Third Avenue and Sixty-Third Street, painted the walls, threw an old carpet on the floor, and voilà!

In 1958, Malachy's was born.

Now, back in those days, even in Manhattan, certain mores and puritanical ways of thinking ruled even in the most progressive barrooms, and certainly in those of Irish extraction. One of those archaic beliefs had to do with a woman who sat unescorted at the bar. For some reason this was considered immoral. Bars then were the dominion of the male of our species, places where men would spend as much time as they could with other men. Today those same macho haunts would be called gay bars, but back then they were male hangouts where homophobia, boasting, tall tales, bullshit, opinions on how to run the country, and liquefied rubbish were the order of the day.

It's been often said that the three most important ingredients for a successful bar are location, location, and location. My partners were bloody geniuses when it came to all three. For one thing, Third Avenue was like an Irish theme park. Every bar was Blarney this or Killarney that. Every window had a huge green neon shamrock with a bright-yellow harp. So Malachy's was a perfect fit. But the most important aspect of the locus of the bar was that it was right around the corner from a habitation called the Barbizon Hotel for Women.

Advertised as the gold standard in safe single-girl living, the Barbizon was twenty-three stories and seven hundred rooms of female pheromones, the largest collection ever assembled in one place. Most of the young women who lived there were blow-ins, Midwestern gals, fed on the farm, pink as the brick of the facing of the hotel, and filled with dreams of stardom, success, or finding Mr. Right. Before they became stars, Joan Crawford, Gene Tierney, Dorothy McGuire, Grace Kelly, Elaine Stritch, Liza Minnelli, Ali MacGraw, Cybill Shepherd, and Candice Bergen all had rooms in the Barbizon. Ronald Reagan's speechwriter Peggy Noonan lived there, as did the unsinkable Molly Brown, who died not in the sea under the *Titanic* but in a Barbizon bedroom in 1932.

It was also home to newly minted Ford models who had not yet settled in Gotham.

Soon after we opened, the girls around the corner started to wander in to be greeted by yours truly and, scandalous as this was at the time, I would suggest they take a seat at the bar. Within no time men were lined up halfway down the block to get in. Malachy's became the first singles bar in New York City, and the cash register was a cacophony of delicious bells and dings.

It was a bar with a fierce amount of drinking and high jinks—a very noisy, very mad place.

The Barbizon had an eleven o'clock curfew. The girls would be home in time but then change into their jammies for the bed check, throw on a raincoat, and sneak down the back staircase and around the corner to Malachy's. Sometimes the girls wore nothing under the slicker. It became a kind of rebellion for them, and we called them "the raincoat brigade." They would stay and drink until three or four in the morning.

On occasion I would escort one of the young darlings back to the hotel. Of course, men were not allowed up in the rooms, but we'd sneak by the matrons at the front desk and make our way up the back stairway. Having fumbled my way to nirvana in bed, I would then dress, descend in the elevator, and boldly doff my cap to the matrons on my way out the door.

At Malachy's, my job was just to be me in full. Free of implanted English snobbery, free of Catholicism, free of the encumbrance of treasure that as poor kids we watched on the movie screens like urchins looking through a window at a Christmas dinner, I filled the bill. I kept the traditional songs and folktales of Ireland alive. This was my calling. I would march into my future with Ireland's beautiful legacy tucked under my arm like a bagpipe.

The only problem was, once the legacy was tucked I would start to drink and begin to wander.

One night I was out on a toot, painting the town with the partners' dough, when I came strolling back to the bar. My associates had hired a new bouncer, which was a development unfamiliar to me. As I strolled to the front of the line, nodded, and tried to get past him, he stopped me with a beefy paw.

"Where do you think you're goin'?"

"Inside."

"You see the line?"

"You see the name on the awning?"

"So?"

"That's me."

"They all say that, backa da line."

Delighted I had been prevented from going to work, I spun on the heels and headed out into the night, where I burnished my credentials as a man-about-town and colorful character.

One night, after a tour of the local hostelries, I found myself placed in the apartment of one Hugh Magill, the time being about half three in the a.m. A quiet time, even in New York, and we were appropriately sipping a nightcap when Magill let loose a torrent of what some people would call obscenities. As they subsided, I queried him on the sudden explosion. It appeared the father of the young woman he was infatuated with, a man from the Main Line in Philadelphia named Roland Roderick Randall (RRR), had decided Magill was not suitable material for his daughter. He had instructed said daughter to break off all communications with my pal. This harsh reaction on Rollie's part struck me as nonsensical despite the facts that Magill drank heavily, worked sporadically, was in and out of various institutions because of his bipolar condition, had difficulty keeping appointments, owned a flaring temper, and pulled wings off butterflies as an adult. On the plus side, he had proper table manners. During his tirade Hugh said he was going to call up RRR and give him the proverbial piece of his momentarily deranged mind. I wrested the telephone from him.

"Better I do it," I said.

And so began the saga of Leftenant Harris Tweed, Royal Air Force, my alter ego.

Why I affected the British accent and assumed a British air navigator's identity I have no idea. It seemed the right thing to do at now four in the morning when drinking.

I identified myself with my nom de guerre to the groggy voice on the line.

"Rollie? I got your number from your daughter, you see, and I'm in Philadelphia, and I intend to come by and stay with you for a few days."

"What do you mean by calling here at this hour of the night?"

"Well, it's not night, Rollie, it's four in the morning, and I understand that you stay up most nights and mornings drinking yourself into a stupor."

"How dare you?" he barked. "I will report you to the British consulate."

"You're not as good a sport as your daughter, Rollie."

And with that he hung up.

From that moment on, and for years to follow, I plagued this man semiregularly with my drunken nocturnal calls. When 4:00 a.m. rolled around, the pressing business of calling RRR took precedence over all other urges. I don't know how I remembered his phone number each time, but I did. Along the way I enlisted a squadron of friends who also adopted names of fabrics to help with the calls. My pal Dick

Hope became Pop Lin; another friend, Sherman Douglas, was Silky Sheen; Tony Hendra was Gab R. Deen; Faye Bricke was Lynn Nin. I believe there were cameos from Mo Hare, Ray On, and Ann Gora.

There were times I called the man collect, and, maybe because I'd awakened him, he was inclined to accept the charges.

My strategy was to launch into some loony story about flying jets over Russia and how the Commies were angry enough to try to shoot me down. I told him that I had been promoted to wing commander and had been awarded the Distinguished Flying Cross, even though I hadn't seen any combat.

At one point a friend who had a contact in the Air Ministry in London secured some RAF stationery, and I sent a pair of boxer shorts, one sock, a used handkerchief, a tattered romance novel, and a blank composition notebook, along with a letter from the air vice-marshal that read:

*It is with my sincere regret that I inform you that Wing Commander Harris Tweed is dead. After a courageous struggle to keep his aircraft aloft, radar lost it near the international date line in the Pacific. If nothing else, Leftenant Tweed will always be remembered as punctual. He left instructions that you should receive all his earthly goods.*

*Godspeed,*
*AVM Terrance "Terry" Cloth*

I sent the package to Rollie.

I let some months elapse before I rang him again at my usual hour to tell him that I wasn't dead after all. I had bailed out of my aircraft and was in a raft surviving on the meat of albatrosses that I whacked with a boat hook. Finally a whaler of Mongolian registry found me alive and well. In fact, I had gained five pounds.

For some reason Rollie allowed the flood of words about my survival before he said anything. When he did speak, he said only, "They let you out again!"

My calls to Rollie stopped only when I quit drinking many years later, and though I might feel a twinge of regret when remembering that behavior, the laughter generated exceeds any remorse.

No one had a better time under the influence than I did.

———

Eventually, though, the aforementioned fear and shame would perch themselves on the shoulders of the once-poverty-stricken alcoholic. These two assassins of serenity never sleep, never take lunch, and never shut up until they kill you. Shame is firmly rooted in your past, and it doesn't matter if it's about the shameful things you did or those that were done to you. And fear is the promise you tell yourself that things will never work out well in future for you. For many of us, this despair of not having a horizon due to the dense darkness we carry leads to deep depression and sometimes self-murder. In the Catholic faith, we were taught that God gave us life and he was the only one qualified to take it away. So suicide means the express train to the overheated habitation of Satan, Beelzebub, the prince of darkness, and all his nephews from the Conservative Party.

I might have had my name on an awning, and in lights on marquees, but those pronouncements did little to assuage the twin assassins shame and fear who, like trained snipers, waited patiently for a clear shot.

In Malachy's one night I met a beautiful, bright young woman who had grown up on Park Avenue and was privileged but not all that happy. Linda's parents had been divorced, which had produced the usual anger and disappointments. We were married fast, had two children fast, and divorced even faster. I was not used to marriage and did not understand that a husband and father ought to get home to participate in domesticity once in a while.

The situation gave the assassins a great store of ammunition, and one night I came up with a brilliant idea to flush them out.

I was in the Hamptons driving on a lonely country road. It was during one of the many times that the marriage was heading for the rocks, and I was out quieting the unnerving thoughts with drink. "Why not?" I whispered to my reflection in the rearview mirror. "Just pull the wheel to the left and head for the trees. No one will ever know, and no one will miss me anyhow."

It was the image of my children, Malachy and Siobhan, that slapped the sense back into me.

It was just a slap, however, and not nearly hard enough for me to exit the road to near annihilation.

The problem was, I knew no other way.

SEVEN

# A Few Last Words

*"I don't think there's any point in being Irish*
*if you don't know that the world is going to*
*break your heart eventually."*

DANIEL PATRICK MOYNIHAN

In 1963 I was involved in running a saloon called Himself on East Eighty-Eighth Street. In those long-ago days I rarely got to sleep before five o'clock in the morning. You never knew who would stroll in the door in the wee hours.

Luckily, my commute was short; I lived in an apartment over the bar. After closing I would lean one shoulder into the wall and use the banister to pull myself up the stairs. There were mornings when the climb felt like ascending Kilimanjaro. With one eye closed I held the key in front of the lock until I was fairly sure the two were lined up, and then with a great thrust I pushed the key toward the meager opening, which, more times than not, seemed to shift locations. Once inside the apartment, I fell into bed as though I were falling off a cliff.

In the soft confines of my nocturnal bunk, I would enter

a land from which I'm surprised I ever returned. My drunken sleep was like a death in a way. There was nothing within, and whatever was happening without didn't matter.

Except this one day.

I was in that particular state of rest early one afternoon when my phone rang with such urgency that not only did it awaken me but I answered the damned thing just to keep the noise from bonging around my cranium.

My lovely Diana was on the phone. The courtship then was fairly new.

"Have you heard the news?" the softest voice in the world inquired, which, of course, I had not.

The date was November 22, 1963.

––––––––

As you might have gathered, I have an interest in all things political in nature. This fascination comes from my impoverished childhood. The view from below is unique. From there it's easy to see that for many high-profile candidates and officeholders the accumulation of knowledge is not a priority, and this has been so, apparently, from time immemorial. In spite of its mastery of literature and language, Ireland has had more than its fair share of political dunces. In the eighteenth century Sir Boyle Roche, a member of the House of Commons, once remarked that half the lies people told about him were not true and the other three-quarters were exaggerated.

"Why should we do anything for posterity?" he once thundered. "What has posterity ever done for us?"

Growing up in Limerick we had Mayor Dan Burke, who would begin each speech with a preamble such as "Let me reiterate what I am about to say."

In *Blaguards* we tell about Burke's campaign to build more public lavatories in Limerick. "And not only should we build urinals for the men," he said, "but we should construct arsenals for the women!"

I've always been fascinated with those who have held the office of the presidency. At this writing the current occupant of the White House is number forty-five, and of that collection eight have died in office, four of whom were assassinated with guns. If you do the math, as they say, you'll find that the death rate in the presidency is 18 percent. That makes holding the highest office in the land, by percentage, the deadliest job in America, topping even logging, fishing, roofing, sanitation work, farming and ranching, steel and iron work, police, firefighting, trucking, working as a telephone lineman, driving a taxi, and all others that make the most-dangerous list.

Of course, most dangerous jobs are imbued with physical risks, while the commander in chief must deal with peril that is more psychological and emotional in nature. Still, a lot of the old farts in the White House died just from being old farts, and Zachary Taylor died from eating cherries and being out in the sun too long.

Some of the tidbits about the US presidency I've accumulated over the years include the last words of presidents:

On his deathbed John Adams purportedly uttered, "Thomas Jefferson still survives." Adams's political rivalry with Jefferson lasted until his final breath, and yet he was mistaken. Jefferson had died four hours before. Though there are differing accounts of Jefferson's last utterance, one version has it that these were his last words: "Is it the fourth?" It was, of course. The rivals both died on July 4, 1826, fifty years to the day from when they had signed the Declaration of Independence.

Teddy Roosevelt's last utterance was, "Put out the light," which wasn't as poetic as it might sound. TR died in his sleep, and his last words were a command to his valet.

Ulysses S. Grant said only, "Water," which you would have said too if you smoked the amount of cigars Grant did.

Lincoln's were, "She won't think anything about it." Mary Todd was worried about what the female guest in the theater box would think about her husband's hand on his wife's just before John Wilkes Booth pulled the trigger.

Another romantic president was James Polk, whose last words were to his wife: "I love you, Sarah. For all eternity, I love you."

Sarah lived for another forty-two years, which is almost an eternity.

On the other side of the spectrum was Zachary Taylor, whose last utterance was, "I regret nothing." You can interpret that statement as you'd like.

Nixon's last word was singular, "Help!" It was too late for him, and in a lot of ways. He had had a stroke and was calling for his housekeeper. Not a very vociferous or memorable send-off for a man who gave us "I am not a crook." I had a radio show during the time Watergate was unfolding. I remember when Dick Nixon dismissed the Watergate special prosecutor, Archibald Cox. On the air one night, I said that where I come from, getting fired is known as getting the sack, which made Nixon a Cox sacker. The quip nearly got me fired from the station.

I always thought his epitaph should have read, "Here Lies Nixon."

All presidents are required to practice the art of lying, which can be called political truth. Moses was the only human in history to break all the Ten Commandments at once by dropping the stone tablets on which they were inscribed. Collectively, it's obvious that the forty-five presidents have broken them all during their time in office. Maybe the most common biblical offense perpetrated by presidents is that of bearing false witness. Imagine if we could somehow stop all politicians from lying about their opponents. With the extra time, we could send an astronaut to Mars and cure cancer, dance with the stars, et cetera.

Lying, of course, is not just the province of presidents and politicians. Any of us given to dreaming are liars in one sense. Some of us do it out of shame or false pride. Coming out of poverty myself, when the occasion presented itself I denied I'd lived in a slum in Limerick and gave a more prestigious address, like on Barrington Street instead of Schoolhouse Lane or Roden Lane. I often boasted that I had gone to university when in fact I had failed the grade school final exam and never had a day in high school. They were lies to be sure. But I wasn't pathological about them. I knew I was lying and why. Besides, they never made me feel any better about myself. But I applied them like salve to a wound that has never really healed. People have said to me that I'm a terrible liar. I respond that I am not a terrible liar, I'm a very good liar. Have been practicing for years. To me a lie is a dream that might come true.

Kennedy's last words came as he rode in the open car in the motorcade in Dallas. "No, you certainly can't," he said in response to the wife of Governor John Connally, who had said, "You certainly can't say that the people of Dallas haven't given you a nice welcome, Mr. President."

The handsome president had been in Ireland a few months before and stopped in Limerick. Some of his mother's clan, the Fitzgeralds, came from Bruff, then a rural village some twenty-five kilometers south. The Fitzgeralds had emigrated to America in the 1840s to escape the Great Hunger. In Limerick, Kennedy spoke at a packed Green Park Race Course that brimmed with pride for the adopted son. He would later say that his trip to Ireland had been one of the happiest times of his life. He promised Limerick he'd be back in the spring with verse:

> Come back to Erin, Mavourneen, Mavourneen, come back aroun' to the land of thy birth. Come with the shamrock in the springtime, Mavourneen.

What Kennedy meant to the Irish and Irish American was more than just pride, more than just the handsome photo that hung in many Irish homes. His ascent to the presidency took away the self-condemnation that was quintessentially Irish. His visit to Ireland legitimized a country that was filled with low self-esteem. Fair, handsome, and witty, he was the dream of every Irish mother and sister. He was the dream of what we

Irish could become. I liked him a lot. Was he the man the Irish thought he was? Of course not. No man could have been.

But he was a war hero, a designation the Irish know something about. Though Ireland itself has never fought in any modern wars, at least in the traditional sense of that horrid word, we've had more than our share of war heroes. Count them. Two hundred fifty-four Irish-born Medal of Honor winners, over two thousand of Irish descent; and more Victoria Cross winners too.

My friend Jim Dwyer wrote a column for the *New York Times* about the preponderance of Irish blood spilled on 9/11—one out of five killed in the terrorist attack had some Irish lineage. Relatives thought they could identify their missing loved ones by the traditional Irish claddagh ring they wore. But so many claddagh rings were found in the rubble that they didn't help much at all. Some of those rings belonged to the firefighters and police officers who charged up the stairs of the towers just before they came crashing down.

———

Earlier that November I had gone to a party at the Pierre, a very high-class hotel in New York. I can't remember what the party was for, some type of social event, but friends had invited me. There I saw the most beautiful woman and went up and asked her to dance. I had met Diana in East Hampton the summer before, and had procured her telephone number. For some reason, however, I hadn't implemented the digits on the dial. On the dance floor I asked Diana to marry me. I guess I was being glib.

We spent most of the party together as I regaled her with my stories and witticisms. My nights on the town had supplied me with a bit of girth. Fully embracing my acting persona, I had let the hair go in the direction it wanted, and my beard was full and blazing red. With a personality as brash as a brass band, I was both a sight to behold and one that was not easy to forget.

Diana was a tad above my social station. Her father was an architect, and her mother an interior designer. She had grown up in Dobbs Ferry and gone to the Professional Children's School in Manhattan, where she studied ballet with Balanchine. Later she majored in English at Smith College. On top of all of that, she was enchanting, a princess from a storybook. The writer Nora Ephron would tell me years later that Diana was one of the most beautiful women she'd ever seen.

As we parted ways that night I knew I was gobsmacked, smitten, bowled over.

On the phone the day Kennedy was shot, I told Diana that we should be together.

I showered, dressed, and hiked my way across town. Diana's apartment was a tiny alcove studio on Riverside Drive. There were only two folding chairs and a bed to sit on. I remember that the rug was red. Her two-year-old daughter slept in a crib in the alcove. Her name was Nina. We sat on the bed and talked about the president and I told her some stories of growing up in Limerick and she told me about herself.

Diana had left her husband because he had become abusive to her after Nina was born. It was then she moved into the little apartment. Nina had something called autism. I didn't know what it meant then, and neither did Diana's mother. When Diana told her on the phone of Nina's condition she'd replied, "Artistic? There's nothing wrong with that."

Diana had brought Nina to a place that specialized in such disorders and there the doctors had told her that her child was a hopeless case and her only choice was an institution. Diana told me she felt very alone. Even her friends tried to protect her from what they called "the burden of Nina." They couldn't understand why a woman would want to take care of her daughter herself.

I asked Diana to marry me again and she laughed. We stayed together that night for the first time. It was the sweetest night of my life. In the morning we took turns caring for Nina. The child couldn't walk, couldn't speak a word, and still ate baby food, which I spooned to her. At first she didn't respond to me at all. But I wasn't about to give up. Autism or no, there isn't a child on this earth immune to my playful silliness. I started singing to her, Irish songs and children's songs. And soon she began to smile and giggle. I told Diana about my uncle Ab and how all of Limerick, it seemed, watched out for him. In Limerick, I told Diana, people like Ab and Nina were just part of life.

I stayed with Diana and Nina for three days. As 9/11 would later be to New Yorkers, it was a time when we needed to be with someone we loved. It was Diana who taught me about love, a word that up until then I'd reserved for descriptions of racehorses and pints of Guinness. We held each other when the judge swore in the man from Texas with the long, sad face as president, when the nightclub manager shot Lee Harvey Oswald on national TV, and when the team of white horses pulled Kennedy's flag-draped hearse to Arlington National Cemetery.

As they did, Jimmy Breslin's words from a column in the newspaper played in my head: "This is a country that has let the art of hating grow so strong that now we kill our Presidents because of it."

As I write this, a maniac, closeted, self-hating gay has just killed forty-nine in a gay nightclub in Orlando. The Black Lives Matter movement protests the number of black men killed by police, and five police officers in Dallas have been shot and killed by a cowardly sniper. So now you can add to the list of haters those who call men and women faggots and dykes and those who despise the good cop just for wearing a uniform, and the killer cops who should be in jail and not in blue in the first place. The hate that killed Kennedy has not gone away and in fact has only gotten worse, it continues to murder over and over again.

Death has no power over hate.

But love does.

The drum-drumming of Kennedy's funeral and the flickering images of John Jr. in his breeches and suit jacket played on a black-and-white TV, but in Diana's apartment there was the loving flow of life.

I knew I was home.

———

And yet there was something in Kennedy's death that made the eternal sleep viable for any of us. Shortly after the president's assassination, the columnist Mary McGrory declared to Daniel Patrick Moynihan that we would never be able to laugh again.

"Heavens, Mary, we'll laugh again," Moynihan assured her. "We'll just never be young again."

Even me, and even in those days and nights when I thought I was bulletproof, I began to ponder what death was like.

Though East Eighty-Eighth Street was thought of as remote then, I had a steady stream of regulars and irregulars who popped into my new saloon, Himself.

So I wasn't at all surprised when one night around closing time two lads I didn't know strolled in. What did surprise me is that they urged a half dozen of us, the bar's habitués, Jack Sanden the bartender, Bob and Ally the waiters, and myself, to step into the back room. We all politely accepted the invitation, primarily because the lads had produced two handguns and pointed them in our particular direction. Compliant, we sat in a semicircle in front of a large mirror that hung on the back wall of the room. One of the armed gents rifled the cash register out front, whilst his companion sat facing us, handgun in hand. At one point the gunman took umbrage at the expression that was apparently affixed to Bob's face.

"Stop looking at me that way," said the gunman, adding "motherfucker" as an exclamation point.

Which, of course, made Bob look in his direction, which further angered the gunman.

"Stop looking at me, motherfucker," said the stickup man, with a bit more emphasis.

Bob, disregarding all his good manners, forced his gaze from the man, but apparently not quick enough for the gent's liking, for he lifted his gun and fired, the bullet whizzing just past Bob's ear and smashing into the mirror, leaving a nice, clean hole with cracks all around.

Next to me sat Ryan, a regular at my saloon, who just minutes earlier had been as drunk as two lords and who was now scared as straight as a Mafia bookkeeper.

"Do you mind if I smoke?" Ryan asked.

"Go 'head," the holdup man answered.

As Ryan reached for the pack in his inside pocket, the sleeve of his jacket moved up a trifle, revealing a watch. Though he hadn't asked us for any of our valuables or money, the gunman took offense at the fact that Ryan hadn't offered.

"Give me that watch, motherfucker," the gunman said.

Ryan duly removed the watch and handed it over.

"Motherfucker, this is a motherfucking Mickey Mouse watch."

Though astonished that the cartoon rodent had done such unspeakable things to his mother, I was not surprised at the style of Ryan's watch. A lighthearted man, Ryan believed the wristwatch suited his personality.

The gunman, however, did not appreciate Ryan's mirth and threw the watch back at him.

Meanwhile, the literal partner in crime came back from the front room, his countenance clenched in a most disagreeable manner.

"There ain't shit in the register," he said.

"They warned me about going into the bar business," said I.

"What did you do with the money?" said he.

Having already been married, and a partner in two

previous saloons, I found the inquiry rather familiar. And so was my answer.

"There isn't any."

The thought of what happened next gives me the shivers still. Under any circumstance, having the muzzle of a revolver pressed to your temple is a disturbing event. But to understand the full impact, as it were, of the moment, you need to know a bit about the time and place.

As it does now, heroin fueled a tidy bit of the crime in the NYC of those days. A few weeks before, just across the street from Himself, a junkie had broken into an apartment and slaughtered two girls, just twenty-one and twenty-three years old. The murders of Janice Wylie and Emily Hoffert are still something of a famous case, not only because of their brutality but also because police arrested the wrong man and beat a confession out of him. The arrest of George Whitmore Jr. was part of the reason behind legislation that brought about Miranda rights. Even I knew the investigation of Whitmore was a bollix from the start. There was a local junkie who came into the bar often to hit me up for a handout, always slavering and trembling. A five-dollar bill then would buy a fix. I felt sorry for the young man and would often give him a pound or two. One day he came into the bar very sick and reached into his coat and pulled out a knife. At first I thought he'd gone bad.

"No, no," he said. "This is the knife from across the street."

"The one from the murders?" At the time the murder weapon was still missing.

"Yes," he said. "Do you want it?"

Because of the proximity of Himself to the crime scene,

detectives on the case were frequently stopping by. I gave the knife to one of them. I knew that nothing happened on Eighty-Eighth Street that my junkie friend didn't know about. If he said the knife was the murder weapon there was a 99 percent chance he was right. Still, George Whitmore was wrongly sent to jail for a crime he didn't commit, and a knife that couldn't have had his fingerprints on it was never heard of again.

So you can imagine that when the lad with the gun told me to tell him where the money was or he was going to blow my head off my shoulders, I took him at his word. There was no gray area, except maybe the stuff in my cranium that he promised to blow across the floor. Cough up the dough, or pow!

I remember that everything stilled. I imagined the process of what would occur. All he had to do was twitch his forefinger an inch toward himself, and a series of swift little events would happen: a piece of forged metal would whack the back of a bullet, causing a small gunpowder explosion, which in turn would send the bullet speeding down the gun barrel, to either end up lodged in my brain or exit clear through, carrying with it small particles of brain matter.

Either way, in the end, I'd be dead.

Over the course of my adult life, I've had the good fortune to survive flights on jet airplanes that had no business taxiing down runways, let alone being tens of thousands of feet in the air. On one of those flights, a nearby cabin door had sprung a leak and threatened to blow off, which would have sucked all of us in coach out into the atmosphere that was streaming

114

by at five hundred miles per hour. After a drunken evening, I missed a flight that ended up in the Bay of Bombay. But this was different. A gun held to your temple is entirely personal, and is something of an evil embrace, a tango of terror.

*The gift of the gab* is a phrase often used to categorize an Irishman's nimbleness with language, but, in fact, it is a pejorative that denigrates the intellect of the Irish people as a whole. Why, I ask, do the Brits speak the King's English, whilst the Irish have the gift of the gab? Seems the worst of a double standard to me. Still, considering the pinch I was in, you could've called my proficiency with the language anything you wanted.

"Look," I said, with as reasonable a tone as I could muster. "Our lives are far more valuable than money, and if there were any here, I would hand the fucking cash over to you."

I think my use of the expletive impressed him. He herded us like a bunch of quivering cows through a doorway and down to the basement, where we promised to stay while he and his cohort made good their getaway, or however the expression goes.

In the immediate aftermath we, in the basement, were like passengers on a great liner the moment after rescue from shipwreck, as it says in a book of which I'm fond. Camaraderie, joyousness, and democracy pervaded the vessel from steerage to captain's table.

Upstairs again, we locked the door, opened bottles, and drank and laughed like the survivors we were.

We had good reason to be grateful. A few nights later the same duo shot and killed a bartender on the East Side.

———————

I would like to blame my ensuing behavior over the next decade or so of my life on my brush with death. I didn't need a reason to drink as if it were Paris before the war, however. The holdup was one of a thousand justifications, but as my friends in church basements say, there is never a reason to drink, only excuses.

———————

Living life in a death-defying manner, however, can have its advantages and can, in fact, improve the company one keeps.

Among the regulars at Himself were Jonathan Winters, Merv Griffin, Phil Harris, and Richard Harris, and laughs were in abundance. The funniest of all of my friends from those days was the aforementioned Pat McCormick. Six foot eight, and at times tipping the scales at 350 pounds while sporting a walrus mustache, Pat was as memorable physically as his humor was unforgettable. If you're of a certain age, you might remember Pat as Big Enos Burdette in the Smokey and the Bandit movies with Burt Reynolds and Jackie Gleason. Pat was a sought-after comic genius and wrote for Phyllis Diller, Johnny Carson, and Steve Martin, just to name a few. Bobby Kennedy hired him to inject some humor into his stump speeches during his tragically short run for pres. Some comedy writers can be boring because their efforts to be funny are so evidently laborious, but such wasn't the case with McCormick.

One day we were driving together up Sixth Avenue in

Manhattan, and as we stopped at a red light, next to us pulled up an NYPD tow truck with a Volkswagen, front wheels airborne, hooked to the back. McCormick got out of the car and knocked on the window of the police vehicle.

"Officer," he said, "I don't know whether or not you know this, but there's a Volkswagen fucking your truck."

When he was asked about Lady Bird Johnson's beautification program for America, he said anything she could do for herself would help.

One night at a dinner he had a bit too much to drink and passed out for a moment or two with his head on the table. When he raised his noggin, I noticed he had a piece of butter stuck on his forehead.

"Pat, why is there a chunk of butter on your forehead?" I inquired.

"I was talking with a dairy farmer who had a bad cough," he said in a split-second response.

McCormick was at his funniest when the subject was death.

I attended his mother's wake, which was a huge gathering of showbiz folk in a funeral home on Lexington Avenue in Manhattan. Pat had some questions for the home's director and asked me to come along for support. Suitably deferential, the director was devoid of humor and the perfect foil for Pat, who asked the man the name of the youngest corpse in the building.

"Why would you want to know that?" the man asked after clearing his throat.

"We have a whole additional room upstairs that we're just

using for flowers, and I thought it would be an excellent idea to challenge his mourners to a volleyball game."

The director looked as if he might choke.

"Put some life in this place," Pat added.

"Oh, no, that would be unseemly," the man said with grave seriousness.

But Pat knew a trout when he had one hooked.

"Well, that's disappointing," says the big man, "but at least there's music on the way."

"Music?" the man croaked.

"Yes," says Pat, "I invited the Duke Ellington Orchestra over for an impromptu set."

If I hadn't pulled Pat out of the office, the director would have needed a coffin himself. No matter how irreverent, how absurd, how extreme, our man would do anything for a laugh. He had all the flowers from his mother's wake shipped to the home of the estranged wife of our mutual friend Tom O'Malley, with a vast amount of condolence cards expressing deepest sympathy.

Pat said he gave up drinking when his liver started setting off airport metal detectors, but he might have given up the spirits a bit too late. He suffered a massive stroke in the late nineties, one that rendered him practically motionless and mute. He lived for the last seven years of his life at the Motion Picture & Television Country House and Hospital in the Woodland Hills neighborhood of LA. Over the years the residents of the actors' home have included Bud Abbott, Curly Howard of Three Stooges fame, and Johnny Weissmuller, who was said to bellow his Tarzan call in the hallways. It was

The brothers at St. John's Cemetery, Queens, New York. A plaque bearing Margaret Mary's name was affixed to the monument, and we spread some of Angela's ashes on the grave.

Margaret Mary's birth certificate

Angela's passport photo, age 17 or so.

Angela (middle) on a beach in Ireland. Frank's first girlfriend is on her right.

Malachy Sr.,
passport photo,
1958 or so.

The bed in our
domicile on
Schoolhouse Lane,
Limerick, Ireland.

Roden Lane. "Buck-
etham Palace," our
communal latrine, is at
the far end.

The lads in second class. I'm first from right, second row.

Leamy's academy of surgeons.

My uncle Ab Sheehan. His obit in the *Limerick Leader* read: "He gave offense to no one."

In the Scouts. The fine strapping lad standing in the middle is self.

On the deck of
*America*. I'm first left,
front row, in the suit
of my dead uncle.

Self in Air Force uni.

The first wife, Linda,
with Siobhan and
baby Malachy.

At the Taj, flanked by
sons Malachy (left)
and Conor.

With Ed Sullivan
and a comedian
whose name now
escapes.

Behind the bar
at Clavin's, I
believe, eyeballing
Tom O'Malley,
the *Tonight Show*
booker.

Step dancing with
Merv Griffin.

Me, Diana, Kathe Green,
and Richard Harris (in
bartender's apron) in front
of Himself, my pub.

The lovely Diana and self,
dressed to the nines.

I always loved to read. *(Photo Credit: Lynn McCourt)*

With producer Bob Rein. I couldn't wait to hear what I would say next.

I forget what the award was for, but it might as well have been "For marrying the most beautiful woman in the world."

Behind the bar as Kevin MacGuinness, my character in the soap *Ryan's Hope*.

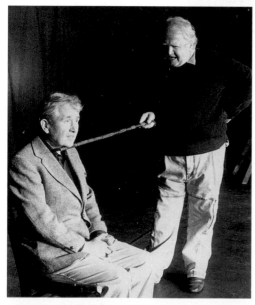

Onstage in *A Couple of Blaguards*.

The brothers and herself. From left: Alphie, Mike, self, and Frank.

Angela on the
blower in my
apartment in
New York.

Taken at my 50th birthday
party. Angela unhooked
herself from the hospital bed
to be there. She died two
months later.

Self at Mungret
Cemetery, where
we placed most of
Angela's ashes.

Cracking up Mario Cuomo, with John Dearie, Tom Dunne, and Joe Crowley. If I remember the line correctly, I said: "Someday Donald Trump will be president."

With President Bill Clinton at an *Irish America Magazine* awards dinner.

Frank's passport photo, age 19.

I loved making the brother laugh.

Co-conspirators in death, Malachy and Brian.

The lady Diana: I will love you forever and more.

At Frank's memorial. From left: self, Bill Clinton, Alphie, and Mike.

The fine actor Tom Berenger with self from the 1990 film *The Field*.

The father with
daughter Siobhan
and granddaughter
Fiona.

The father not
too long before
he died, with
son Cormac in
Belfast.

The McCourt boys.

also at the actors' home that someone might have first uttered one of the most famous adages in all of show business history: "Dying is easy, comedy is hard."

Though the early-nineteenth-century Shakespearean Edmund Kean is most commonly thought of as saying the line, there were some in Hollywood, the actor Jack Lemmon among them, who insisted it was another Edmund who deserves the credit. Edmund Gwenn was also a legendary stage actor, but probably best known for playing Santa Claus in the original *Miracle on 34th Street*. According to Lemmon and others, the director George Seaton regularly visited Gwenn at the Hollywood actors' home and was there when Gwenn was on his deathbed.

"All this must be terribly difficult for you, Teddy," said Seaton, calling his friend by his nickname.

"Not nearly as difficult as playing comedy," Gwenn said, and then died, thereby immortalizing a variance of the famous phrase with his last words.

Others have put their own spin on it. Mel Brooks once said, "Tragedy is when I cut my finger. Comedy is when you walk into an open sewer and die."

Knowing Pat as I did, I'm confident he found something to laugh at, even though he couldn't talk, and I'm sure he did right up until the end.

# EIGHT

# It's a Long Way to Bombay

*This stone was raised to Sarah Ford,*
*Not Sarah's virtues to record—*
*For they're well known to all the town—*
*No, Lord; it was raised to keep her down.*

HEADSTONE,

KILMURRY CHURCH,

COUNTY CLARE

I think it was Dorothy Parker who once said, "Give me heaven for the comfort and hell for the company."

Once when I was in LA pursuing my celluloid dreams, the boss of the American Film Institute, George Stevens Jr., invited me to a party. I didn't know anyone there—A-list celebs filled the place, and I had barely broken into the C-list. But I was putting the drink down pretty good to lubricate the social muscle to insert myself more easily. Working on whiskey number three or four, I spied an older woman sitting by herself, having a cocktail. I went over to say hello.

"I don't know anyone here," I said.

"Does it matter?" she responded.

"At this rate, though, I'll never get anyone to come home with me unless you will."

I thought I was charming and witty, but in hindsight, I had been quite banal.

"Young man," Dorothy Parker said. "If you think you're flattering me, you're not."

Years later I was sitting in Paul O'Dwyer's office. O'Dwyer was a well-regarded New York pol and lawyer whom I've loved spending time with—a funny, wise, and sober man. Unexpectedly, he asked if I knew Dorothy Parker.

"I met her once," I said, and I told him the story.

"Would you like to say hello to her?"

"Yes," I said, "of course."

He turned and took an urn from a drawer.

"Here she is," he said.

By some incredibly random set of circumstances, O'Dwyer had charge of the famous writer's ashes, which he kept in a drawer in his office. Ahead of her time in many regards, Parker was an ardent antiracist and wrote about her feelings about the inequities of race quite often. When she died, in 1967, she left her estate to Martin Luther King Jr. with the provision that if anything happened to the civil rights leader, which of course it did the following year, her estate would go to the NAACP. The NAACP still owns the writer's literary rights. Though Parker left instructions for her estate, and specified her wish to be cremated, for some reason she didn't say anything about custody of her ashes. So for fifteen years they remained in Paul O'Dwyer's cabinet, until the lawyer was finally able to arrange for a burial plot next to NAACP headquarters in Baltimore. With appropriate jocosity, the plaque on the site reads, "Excuse my dust."

———————

Throughout the 1960s and '70s, I acquired enough celebrity to solidify my place as the most famous of the McCourt brothers. No one could pin me down to being anything specific. But I was a well-known commodity on the airwaves as a regular guest on the *Tonight* stage and a frequent visitor to shows hosted by the likes of Merv Griffin, Mike Douglas, and Tom Snyder. You name the talk show of the time and yours truly was a welcomed talker. Later the face of Malachy McCourt was also familiar on the television during the daytime as a soap opera actor on *Ryan's Hope*, *Search for Tomorrow*, *All My Children*, and *One Life to Live*. Angela was particularly proud of my career in daytime drama. Her bingo friends would tickle her to no end when they'd mention they saw me on the television.

"Is that so?" she'd say, with practiced smugness.

As for me, I was particularly proud of my time in the theater. One of the high points of my stage career came when I played Matthew Harrison Brady, the character based on William Jennings Bryan, in a production of *Inherit the Wind*. It was also during that production that I perfected the art of laying curses on people.

I have not only laid curses on people, I've draped them fully to ensure their nonrecovery. I must say, though, there is never any purpose to laying a death wish on anybody, because death brings serenity, great comfort, and peace to all of us, no matter if you're Hitler or Saint Francis. People tend to feel a trifle of disquiet about death, and those who are greedy, evil, and money loving are more fearful than most. So it's best to wish that lot a long, miserable life. It's a puzzle to me that proponents of capital punishment believe that the sentence they've meted out is punishment. To my mind it's not.

But back to curses and the laying of such.

The production of *Inherit the Wind* previously mentioned opened in Scranton, Pennsylvania, in the Lackawanna County Courthouse, and then moved to the Philadelphia City Hall. There we were greeted with great reviews and ran for eight months, which I believe was a record at the time for that city. One of the writers of the play, Jerome Lawrence, came and said it was the best performance he had ever seen. High praise indeed.

I played against type as the Bible-loving prosecutor Matthew Brady, while Jason Miller, who wrote *That Championship Season* and was Father Karras in *The Exorcist*, a role that earned him an Academy Award nomination, starred as the atheist defense attorney, Henry Drummond, based on Clarence Darrow.

Our production caused such a buzz that some Hollywood producer announced that he was going to take it to Los Angeles, where he had visions of not only staging a play but also bringing our version of *Inherit the Wind* to the big screen. He promised that Jason and I would retain our roles, and they would cast the rest in California.

At the time I was a busy lad. After we had closed in Philadelphia, I had to go to Europe for something, and when I
returned, there was an offer waiting for me to do another play.
As I was committed to *Inherit the Wind*, I turned the offer
down. The producer guy hadn't set the rehearsal dates to my
knowledge, so I rang him to get an approximate schedule. His
response was that though they were proceeding with Jason,
he was dropping me from the cast. I was astonished. In a
stammer, I could just barely enunciate the fact that I'd turned
down work.

"Yeah, yeah, yeah," he said. "But we have no contract,
and this is Hollywood, and we need star power, and you're no
star."

I called my union, Actors' Equity, and they said, sorry, you
have no contract, there's nothing we can do. I rang Jerome
Lawrence, and he said he wasn't going to interfere, as the producer knew what he was doing.

So I got to work on the curse. In preparing a curse, it's
essential that you infuse it with energy, direction, and
specificity.

I composed one based on all the numbers in the producer's
life: address, phone, fax, office number, the number of pages
in the script, the number of people in the cast, et cetera. I
wrote the curse and made a huge number of copies. Then I
implemented the plan of sending him the curse once a week.

Almost immediately after implementation, and out of the
blue, Jason Miller called me and said that he wasn't going to
do the play without me, and he pulled out.

I'd called the playwright and told him about the situation,

and he wasn't interested in doing anything about it. So I put a curse on him. Very soon after, his house burned down in one of those California fires.

After receiving several of my hex letters, the producer complained to Equity, and one of its representatives called me to tell me how unprofessional it was for me to put a curse on a producer. As my union was his employer, my first question to him was, "Whom are you representing? The producer or me?"

"You're behaving badly," he said.

"I might be," I said. "But if you don't get off my phone you'll suffer the same fate." I didn't put the curse on him, but not too long after he died anyhow.

In the end the playwright, homeless and singed from my curse, took *Inherit the Wind* back from the producer. I read in *Variety* that the producer's next project was a film based on the life of Sam Walton, the founder of Walmart. I sent him another curse letter with the note that the production would be doomed. To my knowledge he never followed through on the project, and I've never heard of him again.

––––––––––

The downside of applying curses is that they are comprised solely of negative energy. They don't do the person wielding the curse any good, except for the satisfaction you get seeing your enemies suffer. And even though your antagonist is powerless to get back at you, the universe tends to even the ledger out.

In 1956 I was doing a play by Paul Vincent Carroll named *Shadow and Substance* in a theater on Madison Avenue, now the home of a dance school. In the very successful production, I played one of two young curates under the thumb of a domineering priest. An actor named Liam Clancy played the other young priest. One night Liam approached me before the curtain and said he and his brothers, Paddy and Tom, and a guy named Tommy Makem were getting together to record a few songs in a studio in Greenwich Village, and he asked if I would like to come along. Now, I have to say, I'm not now, nor was I ever, a singer, and when I do sing I prove that fact. But neither was Clancy a singer at that point—we were both actors.

"Of course," I said, "I'd love to."

At the time I was married to my first wife, Linda, who was addicted to the makeup. One night we missed an entire affair because she didn't like the way her makeup was going onto the face. But Linda wanted to come along to the studio that night, and I said she could.

When the curtain came down at ten thirty, Liam and I waited outside the theater for Linda to show. After a half hour or so, and no Linda, I told Liam to go ahead and that I would meet him at Sheridan Square in Greenwich Village. Eleven thirty came and went, as did twelve midnight. Finally at twenty to one in the a.m. Linda shows up with a makeup excuse. I knew at that point that Liam and the boys wouldn't still be waiting for me in Sheridan Square, and I also realized I didn't know the location of the studio.

I shrugged, no song for me, and home I went with Linda.

Meanwhile the recording session in Greenwich Village gave birth to an Irish singing group called the Clancy Brothers and Tommy Makem. They would go on to sell albums in astronomical numbers, tour the world many times, and become beloved by millions and millions of fans, all of which might have included me if the wife's makeup had done what it was supposed to do.

———

For years I had talk shows on both television and radio. I helped perfect the art of bullshit now called talk radio as a pioneer talker for WMCA here in New York.

But I began with a television talk show in 1969. It was then I had the privilege to interview Muhammad Ali, who died a few months before this writing, in case you were on the moon and didn't hear. His Parkinson's disease inexorably destroyed that once-amazing body, the image of which was displayed via every conceivable media outlet. Crocodile tears flowed from hypocritical eyes for the great loss of humanity that came with Ali's death. Many of those same eyes had blazed with rage and hate when the champion boxer told America that he would not join its army, wear its uniform, carry its guns thousands of miles to kill little brown people who had never done anything to him. Not a single Vietcong had been involved in enslaving his progenitors. Not one North Vietnamese citizen had called him a nigger. Ho Chi Minh had not hanged any of his ancestors from trees.

Many of those who cried at such volume when he died were the same ones who had decided to put him in jail for having the nerve not to kill or get killed by people he didn't know.

Having access to some dollars from thumping other human beings, he took his case to the Supreme Court, and surprisingly it agreed he ought not to be forced to fight and murder strangers whom he was not likely to meet in his normal life.

On my show Ali's presence was more than formidable. Indeed, an aura filled the space around him. Not only was he one of the most graceful human beings, but also his light, eloquent manipulation of the English language was almost as dazzling as his physical prowess.

One of the reasons I was successful on the radio and television was my lack of the verbal editor most people have in their brains. When a thought wanders through my cranium, more times than not it finds its freedom past my teeth and through the slot in my face commonly called the mouth. This ability, if you can call it that, thrilled me to no end. I simply could not wait to hear what I had to say next.

I told Ali that I knew that his great-grandfather came from County Clare in Ireland. One Abe Grady, I said, emigrated from Ireland to Kentucky, where he married a freed slave who would give birth to Ali's grandmother, who in turn would give birth to Odessa Grady, the boxing champ's mother. My statement brought an unusually strong response from Ali. At the time he was the face of the Black Muslims and, at last count, there aren't many Black Muslims in Ireland, so his white lineage might have diminished his standing in that community.

He left the set after his segment with barely a good-bye to yours truly and made his way to the airport for a flight to Chicago. I thought I had made an enemy of him for life. The next night we were readying for the first guest of the evening when a young African American man showed up on the set. I remembered him as one of Ali's entourage. Ali had sent him all the way from the Windy City with a message for me. The man said Ali wanted to apologize for leaving the show so abruptly and without thanking me. "Mr. Ali wanted me to tell you that you know more about him than he knows about himself," the young man said. His great-grandfather had indeed been Irish, the great fighter said, and had been, from what he knew of him, a fine man.

They said Ali died from respiratory failure, which is a layman's term that means he stopped breathing and exhaled his spirit into our universe. Although the image of his fists of rage is imprinted on magazine covers and in memories, it was not anger he left behind but forgiveness for those who had wronged him.

Sometimes I wonder if I can do the same. Anger is the last great mountain to forge over to get to the green field of serenity, especially when the store of anger you hold feels almost ancient, because it's been with you forever. I think forgiveness is the key to eternal happiness. Not some God Guy forgiving us, but our forgiveness of others. And of ourselves. Easier said than done, though.

During most of this time when I was on the stage, or in front of a camera or radio microphone, brother Frank was toiling in anonymity as the teacher of thousands of high school students at Stuyvesant High School in Lower Manhattan. But though our paths seem disparate, we remained close. Much of that bond, perhaps, came from what we had survived as children, but it came also from living in the big, great city of New York. Limerick was a small town compared to the Big Apple, and we held on to each other so as not to be washed to sea by the flow of people.

Though we talked nearly every day on the phone, we tried to make the faces meet as often as possible. One of the more favored places where that occurred was the Head, as we called the Lion's Head, a bar of some renown on Christopher Street in Greenwich Village.

Frank might have been the first of us to discover the Head. At one point, between marriages, he was living in Brooklyn Heights, and one of his neighbors was Paddy Clancy from the Clancy Brothers. Paddy brought Frank to the Head the first time.

The writer Joe Flaherty once said that "good saloons combine the best aspects of the womb and the coffin." He might have been talking about the Head, where he was a fervent habitué although he had given up drinking years before. The Head would change the very direction of Frank's life. But even in the years before he met his wife Ellen there, the Greenwich Village saloon was our solace, our salvation in the nuthouse that was our lives. I know, of course, that there can be too much of a good thing, and I spent far too much time in saloons. But until you reach the jumping-off (as in jumping off a building) point, a saloon can do what a thousand hours of therapy can't.

The Head wasn't the first bar where we received analysis. The White Horse Tavern, made famous by the poet Dylan Thomas, preceded the Head as our therapist's couch. There Frank and I became friendly with another Dylan, though he went by the name Zimmerman at the time. Bobby was just a kid of eighteen from Minnesota, hanging out with a guitar and singing in the back room with the Clancys, who also made the White Horse their home away from home. Even then you could tell there was something special about Bob Dylan—"I don't write songs," he once said. "I just write them down."

One night Frank and I brought the mother to the Head. She was living in Brooklyn at the time, I think. Some woman at the bar began to pontificate about the sanctity of life, and how all living things, from pigeons to people, were worthy of our respect. Even plants, she said, have a life force, not unlike our own, and should be talked to.

"Do you talk to your plants?" she asked the mother.

"No," Angela told her. "I live alone."

After Dylan Thomas had drunk himself to death there, the White Horse became a destination for curiosity seekers and tourists, and that's when Frank and I looked for a new therapist.

Though closed now over twenty years, the Lion's Head

was once home to newspapermen like Pete Hamill and Jimmy Breslin, boxers like José Torres, and tough-guy actors like Jack Warden. While queens and transvestites paraded down Christopher Street in those closeted 1960s, the Head's smoky, dark barroom was a bastion of burly, hard-drinking, women-chasing men. It wasn't all male, however. Before she became a famous actress, Jessica Lange worked there as a waitress. It was our type of place. In an interview with the newsman Jack Newfield, Mario Cuomo once credited me with saying, "The Irish go to the Lion's Head to think like Jews, and the Jews go there to learn to drink like the Irish." I don't remember saying it, but the line is apt.

Along with the Clancys and Joe Flaherty, Frank and I would lead sing-alongs in the back room. One of the more spirited renditions would come when some favored son of the Head would meet his untimely, or timely, death. It was then we'd sing "Will Ye Go, Lassie, Go?" which for some unknown reason became the dirge for the Head's departed.

> If my true love she were gone
> I would surely find another
> Where wild mountain thyme
> Grows around the blooming heather.
> Will ye go, lassie, go?

Even before the world knew it, I knew that Frank was a celestial talent formed by listening to a sometimes-sober father who was a master at the story himself, and by soaking in every detail of a childhood unlike any other. Frank's worldview was quintessentially Limerick, a witty sorrow that found laughter even in defeat. Especially in defeat.

In *Angela's Ashes* Frank tells a story about reading a composition he wrote in the fifth grade. The assignment that Puddledy O'Dea gave him was to imagine if Jesus grew up in Limerick instead of Nazareth:

This is my composition. I don't think Jesus Who is Our Lord would have liked the weather in Limerick because it's always raining and the Shannon keeps the whole city damp. My father says the Shannon is a killer river because it killed my two brothers. When you look at pictures of Jesus, He's always wandering around ancient Israel in a sheet. It never rains there, and you never hear of anyone coughing or getting consumption or anything like that and no one has a job there because all they do is stand around and eat manna and shake their fist and go to crucifixions.

Anytime Jesus got hungry all He had to do was walk up the road to a fig tree or an orange tree and have His fill. If He wanted a pint He could wave His hand over a big glass and there was the pint. Or He could visit Mary Magdalene and her sister, Martha, and they gave Him His dinner no questions asked and He'd get his feet washed and dried with Mary Magdalene's hair while Martha washed the dishes, which I don't think is fair. Why should she have to wash the dishes while her sister sits out there chatting away with Our Lord? It's a good thing Jesus decided to be born Jewish in that warm place because if he was born in Limerick he'd catch the consumption and be dead in a month and there wouldn't be any Catholic Church and there wouldn't be any Communion or Confirmation and we wouldn't have to learn the catechism and write compositions about him. The End.

When Frank finished, Puddledy looked at him very oddly. "Did your father write this composition, McCourt?"

"No, sir."

"You wait here then."

Puddledy left with the composition, and after some time he came back with Hoppy O'Halloran, the headmaster.

"Did you write this composition?" Hoppy asked.

"I did," said the brother.

What was said next Frank didn't remember, but I do, as I was sitting in the classroom that day. This was when Frank had been left back a year because of the typhoid fever.

"McCourt, you are a literary genius," Hoppy said. "What you have to do is leave this country and go to America. They'll love you there."

When Frank met Ellen in the Lion's Head he found true love, which allowed him the freedom and confidence to write his literary masterpiece. It took fifty years for it to happen, but Hoppy was right.

————

As for holding on to my spot as the best-known McCourt, well, the position had its drawbacks. For one thing, the

134

work wasn't steady. In fact, the more I drank, the less stable it became. After my first marriage had dissolved, I found myself more gray than colorful. I was also broke, and this is a deadly combination that can drive men to great lengths of insanity.

Such was the case when a fellow with whom I was vaguely familiar presented me with an unusual business opportunity that would involve far-flung travel. The adventure started innocently enough, a conversation in a saloon. How many wild schemes are hatched within arm's length of the beer tap, only to disappear like foam off a stout? But it seemed the perfect escape from the nattering guilt and shame I had about my failed marriage, about Malachy and Siobhan. The thing is, though, you can't run from your problems. If you have a broken leg in New York, you're going to have a broken leg in Europe, or wherever you go. If you have a broken heart in New York, it's still broken in Paris.

I was directed to the Wall Street area the next day, where I was to meet my man with instructions.

We sat in a nearly empty coffee shop in the middle of the afternoon. The man was dressed in a gray suit and wore spectacles. He was nondescript except for the cleft palate, which made his speech almost impossible to not find humorous.

"What's the job?" I asked.

"Nu have ta muggle in tum gold."

"To where?"

"Mumbay."

His words were like shish kebab to a starving man.

He told me to go to the Indian consulate to secure a visa

and handed me an airline ticket to Zurich, where I would arrange a connecting flight.

I immediately went out and got fluthered to celebrate my new venture and lost the airline ticket to Switzerland. Your man was infuriated, but bought me another. I was singing when I boarded the plane, and when they told me they weren't going to serve me any booze I threatened to sing all the way to Zurich. That did the trick. Soon I heard the clink of the little airline bottles heading my way.

In Zurich I checked into the prescribed hotel. There a man arrived to meet me with a suitcase filled with gold and a length of canvas that he fashioned into a corset with twenty pockets, each one big enough to hold a kilo of gold bars.

Laden with the bullion, I flew from Zurich to Rome, then on to Bombay.

My God, Bombay. What a city.

"What is the purpose of your visit?"

"Tourist."

"Welcome to India."

At the time gold was seventy dollars an ounce in India and only thirty-five dollars an ounce in the rest of the world. So there was a good chunk of money to be made.

I had trouble getting in touch with my contact. Our man in New York had given me a phone number that I called for three days straight without luck. I was about to go mad. On the fourth day, finally, a voice came on the line.

"'Ello?"

"This is Haji Kahn," I answered, using my code name.

"Meet me tonight at the Gateway of India."

So it was off to the Gateway and the disposal of the bullion.

It was dark and hot, and the body was soaked with perspiration due to the gold-laden vest. I waited there in the gloom until a man approached.

"Haji Kahn?"

"Yes."

"Follow me."

He began to run, loping along with me struggling to keep up.

We got to our destination. I was never so happy in my life as when I finally got rid of that golden burden that encased my body.

Had I been caught, the sentence was an automatic five years. And it wouldn't have been in some country-club jail like the ones for white-collar crime we have here in America. It would have been in a diseased and parasite-infested hellhole.

While I was in Bombay, I took to following the early-morning funeral processions to the crematoriums. I felt comforted by the song and the dance. In one, the song had the primordial strain of stringed vinas and sitar. All of a sudden, it began to morph into something familiar, or at least it sounded that way to my ears. I began to sing along; it wasn't an Indian song that honored the dead at all. At least not to my ears.

It's a long way to Tipperary.
It's a long way to go.
It's a long way to Tipperary,
To the sweetest girl I know.

The whole mourning party looked back at me, this lunatic with a mane of burning red hair and a wild red beard, half-pissed at two in the morning, his voice gaining momentum with each step.

Good-bye, Piccadilly,
Farewell, Leicester Square,
It's a long, long way to Tipperary,
But my heart's right there.

They began to clap and laugh, thinking I was singing this great mourning song, not knowing that it was a British occupation song.

I made six gold-smuggling trips, carrying twenty kilos of the precious metal each time. I was so lonely and miserable, and drinking so much, that I didn't care if I got caught or not. And because I didn't care, I didn't get caught.

I also didn't care if I lived or died. So, of course, I stayed alive.

# NINE

# I Come from a Long Line of Dead People

*"I want to die like my father, peacefully in his sleep, not screaming and terrified, like his passengers."*

BOB MONKHOUSE

By the time I reached my fifties, the only tangible things I had learned about death and its hereafter were not to believe the Catholic Church's explanation, and that the cost of dying can keep you awake at night, which ultimately will kill you.

For the upper class, there's a funeral home on the Upper East Side of Manhattan with the warm, friendly name Frank E. Campbell's, and for over one hundred years Campbell's has been the only place to go when you have to go. Among the notables who made Campbell's their last appearance were Mae West, Judy Garland, mobster Frank Costello, Joan Crawford, John Lennon, the Notorious B.I.G., Phyllis Diller, and Philip Seymour Hoffman.

For a story she did for the *New Yorker*, writer Patricia Marx walked into Campbell's with a turtle to inquire if she could prepay for final arrangements for the slowpoke.

"But it will outlive us all," said the nervous funeral home representative.

Then there is a bar on the northern edge of the Bronx called Rory Dolan's, and an excellent establishment Rory's is. Customers there are many, and on any given night the registers ring frequently and rhythmically. That said, if it weren't for the steady stream of mourners from the funeral homes along McLean Avenue, Rory's might have gone the way of the saloons that once boasted my name above the doorway. People die, but business is alive and well at Rory Dolan's and many other similar blue-collar watering holes that cater to the working dead.

> The working class can kiss my arse,
> I've got the foreman's job at last.

———————

Whether in the Bronx or on Madison Avenue, however, one thing remains: the need for the wallet when bidding your loved ones the final good-bye.

The cost of a funeral is excessive. Especially for those with fame. They say that Elvis's funeral cost over $23,000. All of that cash couldn't change the fact that he was dead. One of Elvis's distant cousins snapped a photo of him, pasty and slack jawed, in the coffin, a picture that found itself on the cover of the *National Enquirer,* which sold some 6.5 million copies. Death sells.

Princess Diana's send-off cost five mil, and 2.5 billion watched on TV. A million witnessed in person the funeral procession to Westminster Abbey, where Elton John sang "Candle in the Wind 1997."

The patron saint of fiscal conservatism, Ronald Reagan, had a funeral that some say cost taxpayers a fortune. Reagan's national day of mourning closed the stock market, preempted network television shows, and gave federal workers a paid day off. The price tag for the feds taking the dead day alone was $400 million. How's that for trickle-down economics?

Even for us average citizens, death and debt are synonymous. With all the trimmings, a wake and funeral today can soar to eight grand or more.

There are ways to cut corners.

There was this fellow who played the bagpipes for New York City's Department of Sanitation's Emerald Society Pipes and Drums band. Along with marching in parades, our man, Pat we'll call him, had a thriving side business performing at funerals. So good was his part-time gig that just about every time Pat's phone rang somebody was dead, which was the case when the call came that a gal named Bridget Flynn, who had lived in Yorkville for every day of her ninety-eight years, had died.

The funeral was held at Saint Francis de Sales, a church that has occupied its spot on East Ninety-Sixth Street for over a hundred years. The morning of the funeral was one of those hot summer mornings when heat rises like microwaves from the sidewalk. When Pat arrived he was already sweating profusely in his kilt and gear, and he was discomforted further by the Con Ed workers who were in the process of unearthing a portion of the sidewalk and street in front of the church. In Pat's mind he was as much a musician as a sanitation specialist, and the idea of playing over the jackhammers irritated his artistic sensibilities. Besides, there was no way the family would go for the extra cost of "Danny Boy" when they couldn't even hear him play "Amazing Grace," which came with the package.

Now, even though investors fund Con Ed and not taxpayers, there exists a camaraderie between the utility and city agencies such as the Sanitation Department, for in the outer boroughs— as once in Yorkville—no shame is seen in working for either. So when the piper explained the situation, the men in orange vests and yellow plastic earmuffs were happy to take a blow.

The funeral went off in the appropriate hush. The almost centenarian had outlived most of her friends, and yet there was a modest gathering of children, grandchildren, great-grandchildren, nieces and nephews, and the like, all dark haired and fair skinned just as Bridget had once been when an elevated subway train rattled over Third Avenue. When Pat played the procession out of the church, there wasn't a dry blue eye in the lot.

Though the Catholic Church had softened its stance against the practice (before 1963 it was expressly prohibited), the hierarchy of the faith has never completely embraced the practice of cremation. The idea behind the prohibition was that Christ needs a whole body to levitate when the world comes to an end and he won't be able, the thinking went, to put all the ashes together. Of course, this reasoning discounts the dusty state of a body that has been in the ground a thousand years or so. Ashes to ashes, dust to dust, as they say. If you ask me, and no one will for some reason, I think they're all in it together: the Church, the funeral directors, the people who sell you the cemetery plots, the newspaper obit writers, the lot of them.

Despite their mother's allegiance to the Holy Mother Church, and in spite of its displeasure at such a practice, Bridget's family chose cremation, mostly because it's cheaper than digging a hole in Queens. So instead of carrying a coffin, her oldest took the urn down the steps of Saint Francis de Sales. These were the same steps that Bridget was carried up by her father to be baptized. The same ones she was whisked down the day of her wedding. The steps that were the perch from which she watched Ronald Reagan eulogize an old chum named Jimmy Cagney who had grown up with her in the parish. And, as the years piled one on top of the other, the same steps she climbed at an ever-decreasing speed to attend Mass each day.

Perhaps it was in thinking of the innumerable times his mother had climbed the four marble steps that the idea came to the son carrying her ashes. Pat had stopped playing, and the jackhammers had begun again. A barroom whisper from son to bagpiper to Con Ed worker relayed the request. The same practiced shrug that has sealed deals between working New Yorkers forever answered said request.

A Con Ed worker lowered Bridget's urn into the chasm opened by the jackhammers. Sometime after lunch, but before 4:30 p.m. quitting time, a combination of crushed stone, sand, reinforced steel, and water would be mixed, poured, and troweled, sealing it as tight as the best Italian mausoleum.

There she rests today, and if you ever take the M96

crosstown and pay close attention, you can feel the bump of her rent-free residence just east of Second Avenue in front of Saint Francis de Sales.

———————

In 1981, at the end of her holiday visit to the USA, one that lasted twenty-three years, the mother, Angela, was in Lenox Hill Hospital dying from the ravages of cigarette smoking, which had destroyed her lungs. She had started the deadly habit, according to herself, at about the age of thirteen, and must have smoked thousands of the fags called Woodbine over the next fifty years, cutting her lungs' ability to access the air that is entirely free and accessible. She lingered at Lenox Hill Hospital for several months, all the while complaining that they were prolonging her now very uncomfortable life. When I asked her if she wanted to be buried or cremated, she said, "Surprise me."

She complained to me that abortions were allowed, but they would not help people die in peace. One doctor suggested to her that she live out her remaining life in a nursing home.

"No one lives in a nursing home," the mother said. "You barely exist there."

I discussed letting her die with a doctor who invoked ethics and law as obstacles to sending her off. Sometimes we don't know where words come from, but out they come. "Don't worry, Doctor," I said. "We come from a long line of dead people." He looked at me like a man just bitten in the testicles by a rabid rat, his eyes moving swiftly from one side to the other, seeking escape, which he did down the hall, leaving me with one hand raised and trying to remember the word *euthanasia*, which means *a good death*.

At one point a priest came in and offered her some religious comforts, and Angela informed him that the Church had been entirely absent in the days when she could've used it, and that now that she was at the end of her life she did not need any of the Church's help. The priest was followed by a psychiatrist who hopped in to talk to her about how she felt. After a bit of chat, he expressed the opinion that the mother was depressed.

"How long did you spend in school to come up with that one?" the mother asked. "I can't breathe, have a bad heart, a broken hip, and spend every hour of every day lying in a hospital bed gasping for breath. I can barely move. I think you're right. I am depressed."

Various bingo buddies arrived. With cheery optimism they would assure Angela that she'd be up and about by Christmas, and, in fact, she somehow pulled herself out of the hospital bed with the intake of oxygen and pills and got into a wheelchair to attend my fiftieth birthday party. Though the mother knew better than anyone, even the doctors, how dire her situation was, part of her wanted to believe that she would survive. Then the reality would creep back in and she would become sorrowful. I had to tell her friends not to talk about her getting better and just understand that she was dying and to say good-bye.

Very quietly one night, one of the nurses came in and removed the various tubes and needles, took off Angela's rings, and gave them to me. Alphie and Frank had done their shift on the deathwatch, and it was my turn. At about 2:00

a.m. Angela emerged from her twilight sleep, opened one blue eye, and addressed me.

"What are you doing here?" she asked.

"I thought you might die tonight."

"I might and I might not, but that's my business," she said. "Why don't you go home to your bed."

"Are you sure you want me to go?"

"Yes," she said. "Go home."

She then closed her eye, thus dismissing me, and I left. Not a couple of hours later I received the call from the hospital that she had died.

––––––––––

Frank, Mike, and self were severely deficient in the money department, so it fell to the brother Alphie to pick up the tab at the funeral home. At the time Alphie owned a successful Mexican restaurant called Los Panchos. The Spic-Mick, we disrespectfully called him. Frank, Alphie and his wife Lynn, Diana, and I all went to said funeral home and met up with the death profiteer. We sat in a semicircle in stiff chairs in front of a large oaken desk, behind which he sat with his fingertips together like the arch of a church. The polish on his fingernails seemed to glimmer. He had golden hair, a gold watch, and a gold tie pin, and his smile, which made it look as though he was experiencing some painful gas, revealed a gold tooth. I leaned into brother Frank.

"This is going to cost Alphie," I whispered.

Of course came the well-practiced condolence, the hushed tone, the pained smile, the lowering of the eyelids.

The director murmured a few phrases about our loss and the importance of a dignified death, from which he deftly pivoted into his sales pitch. Out came the laminated binder with the high-glossy photos of every conceivable kind and make of coffin. There were themes for baseball fans, duck hunters, and fly-fishers. I imagined Angela spending all eternity looking up at a largemouth bass. Choices came in mahogany, walnut, cherry, maple, oak, pecan, poplar, and pine. There were bronze, copper, and stainless steel for long-lasting "better protection," the funeral director said, which brought images of worms and eye sockets. I can't remember whether or not our man showed us the deluxe Promethean back then, but when the King of Pop, Michael Jackson, died some years later, he was buried in the twenty-four-carat gold-plated sarcophagus known as the "golden send-off," which presumably came without a golden shower.

That didn't seem to be the case with us. "You'll want the teak," the director began, "with the gold handles and the blue satin lining. The pillow that comes with this set is silk."

At the time, negotiators had just settled a sanitation strike in NYC, and an army of satisfied sanitation workers were clearing the mountains of smelly garbage from sidewalks and streets.

"Do you think we could just purchase a body bag?" I asked. "We'll put her out on the heap in front. They'll collect her."

Our man behind the desk looked as though he were passing a kidney stone and was most relieved when we told him we'd take the bargain coffin and we left. "There's a man that has twenty years of extreme unctuousness," Alphie said as he did.

Mother Angela would get the cremation package, which

was a step up from what she had desired. "Just throw me in River Shannon and let me float away," she once said. The Shannon was what she missed most of all about Ireland when she was in America.

We followed the usual path one takes in preparing a loved one's departure. We put notices in the local newspapers, got Angela into the coffin and into the viewing area, and waited for friends, family, and assorted bodies to arrive and have a look.

The funeral parlor was on West Seventy-Second Street in Manhattan. The chairs were set very formally in rows. We immediately put them in a circle, and someone went out and bought beer.

Drink was taken, and a sing-along began, much to the astonishment of management and visitor alike. Alphie has the best voice in the McCourt family, so he led the refrain, with Frank admirably accompanying him on the harmonica, at which the brother was more than proficient.

We first sang the songs we knew Angela disliked, and if she were not dead she would've arisen and smote us:

Good-bye, Johnny dear, when you're far away,
Don't forget your dear old mother far across the sea;
Write a letter now and then and send her all you can,
And don't forget where'er you roam that you're an
Irishman.

But we ended with our version of "Barefoot Days," the family's anthem.

I can remember how proud I used t' be
When Dad an' Mother would buy new shoes for me
Now, that's the feeling we've all had
How new shoes would make you glad
But the best time, if you recall
When you wore no shoes at all

When *Angela's Ashes* was published and began to become quite familiar to people around the world, stories about the mother's ashes and their whereabouts began to appear in various publications and informal conversation. Most of the stories about them in the press were untrue.

Frank didn't help matters any. I was always under the impression that the title came from the mother's Woodbine fags. But Frank told an interviewer that the story of Angela's cremation ashes was in the original manuscript and had been edited out to be used in his second memoir, *'Tis*.

I don't have anything against a good lie. But some of the ones that made their way into newspapers offended even my elastic sense of the truth.

Now, they say it's not nice to speak ill of the dead, but I believe there is no better time—they can't talk back.

So here goes.

As you might remember, Richard Harris was an acclaimed actor and, from his Academy Award–nominated role in *This Sporting Life* to his portrayal as Dumbledore in the Harry Potter movies, a bona fide international movie star. He shone on the big screen for nearly forty years. Like me, Richard grew up in Limerick, though we didn't mix. He was from a prominent, well-off family and went to the Crescent Jesuit School, and I was a Laner, the lowest of the low and barefoot much of the time.

We became friendly here in America, though I played rugby against him in 1950 in Ireland. It was an "under twenty" league. Harris was a year older than I, so he was born in 1930, which means he was a cheat. So were many of his mates. Ringers filled the team.

We became close drinking buddies (a contradiction in terms) in New York when I ran Malachy's and, later, Himself. When Harris would come into town, I would know I was in for a bender, a fight, and a hangover of epic proportions.

One night in a pub, a few of us, Frank and myself included, were having a heated discussion on a forgotten subject when Harris put his hand to Frank's face. "What the fuck do you know," he said contemptuously, "you're just a schoolteacher." Frank's reaction was to lash out with his fist and break the actor's nose. Later, when Harris retold the story, he emphasized that Frank threw the punch and ran, which was not the case. Though you wouldn't blame him if he had; Frank was at least fifty pounds lighter than Harris, who was still in terrific shape. Cowardice, however, wasn't in the brother's character. Myself and a few of the boys did usher him out the door so as not to tempt fate, but Frank did not run.

Harris was a revisionist. He played Oliver Cromwell, the hero of the eponymous movie, with an over-the-top vigor that left little doubt of what a progressive spirit and great champion of the common man old Oliver was. Of course, easily dismissed in the film was the fact that Cromwell laid siege to the city of Drogheda, Ireland, in mid-seventeenth-century Ireland, slaughtering three thousand men, women, and children.

The English Parliament declared a national thanksgiving day in celebration and, in its official record, wrote, "This House of Parliament does approve of the execution done at Drogheda as an act of both justice to them, the butchered ones, and mercy to others who may be warned by it."

The day of the Drogheda massacre happened to be September 11, a eerie precursor of another horrible day to come. But Cromwell's killing of innocent Irish didn't stop there. His forces would kill thousands more in Wexford, and then five thousand Limerick citizens the following year. According to Harris, Frank besmirched the reputation of his hometown in *Angela's Ashes*, but he must have thought that his own portrayal of the mass murderer of Limerick was pure art.

---

Dickie Harris was always bragging about the size of his penis, a boast that I paid little mind to but that seemed to tickle a couple of gay lads who were always hanging around him. Now, I'm a staunch supporter of the LGBT community and back up my words by marching each year in the only really inclusive and gay-friendly Saint Patrick's Day parade in New York—held, aptly, in Queens. But I'm not a fan of those who talk a straight game only to be bent in secret. Harris was always going on about what a great seducer of women he was.

One time, in what he pretended was a slip of the tongue, he mentioned that he screwed Princess Margaret.

Actions, however, speak louder than words.

After he had divorced his first wife, the daughter of a peer who sat in the House of Lords, Harris decided to career around Europe in a private plane with a few pals, including yours truly. We flew all over the place—Paris, Copenhagen, Hamburg, Stockholm, and Rome—and hardly spent a sober day or night. One particularly painful morning, he sheepishly asked me if he had made a pass at me the night before. I was astonished, but there was something latent in his words, as if they revealed his biggest secret, and one that he hoped he would take to his grave.

"Are you joking?" I asked.

"Forget about it," he answered, and walked away.

I've never forgotten that moment.

With his publishing success, Frank not only supplanted me as the most famous McCourt but replaced Richard as Limerick's most famous former citizen. This sent Harris nearly cuckoo. Blind with jealousy, the actor went on an Irish radio station and called Frank the most bitter human being he'd ever met in his entire life. He said that Frank's Pulitzer was a "common prize." What's more, he said, Frank hated him because the actor was so successful, which was patently untrue. Frank didn't care about Harris enough to hate him. And Frank didn't have a jealous bone in his body.

Dickie's envy toward my brother peaked with his tale about our mother's ashes, a lie he spread every chance he had.

He said that Frank and I went to him to borrow money to ship the ashes back to Ireland. Instead of using the money for the shipping, we went out on a bender and left the ashes in a bar in Queens. When we finally got them back, we had them shipped by a fly-by-night outfit that lost the mother's ashes at Kennedy Airport, where they remained, unclaimed, in some lost-and-found office.

Harris told interviewers that he knew Angela from Limerick and that she was a staunch Catholic and would never have agreed to be cremated.

When you're as poor as we were, you either glorify the Church or blame it, and the mother was squarely in the second camp. He knew nothing of my mother, and only as much about Frank and me as you can see through the bottom of a pint glass.

———————

I had a part in the dysfunctional nature of my relationship with Dickie Harris. We drank buckets together, and I never once tried to hold him back. I'm sure I wasn't the best influence. We had some good, rollicking times. In 2002 I heard that he was laid low with the cancer and was in a hospital in London. I happened to be in London at the time, but the newspapers said he was recovering. I didn't go to see him. I also thought he might become abusive. But I was shocked and saddened when I read that he'd died and that I'd missed my chance to see him off. I've always felt sorry about that.

Dickie Harris could be hilarious and, as I understand, was so to the end. Before he was hospitalized, he was living in a £2,000-a-week suite at the Savoy Hotel in London. The story was told that when the ambulance men were moving him on the gurney, they were asked not to take him through the front door, so they had to push the gurney through a packed dining room. In the middle of the crowd eating dinner, Harris raised himself up on his elbows and shouted, "It was the food!"

—————

The actual story about Angela's ashes is nothing like Harris's version, though they didn't get the first-cabin treatment. Frank took the can of ashes from the crematorium and brought them home to his apartment, where they stayed until he married wife number two. Then, in 1985, Frank and self were booked to perform our play, *A Couple of Blaguards*, in Limerick. Over the years, we'd talked now and then about spreading the ashes on the Sheehans' plot in Mungret Cemetery. We decided to do just that on the trip. Frank had gone ahead of me, so I had to go to his apartment building's basement and root through his belongings to find the tin can that held the remains of the mother.

That was the easy part. Not being flush, I booked Diana and self on a charter flight to Shannon. The tickets were almost too inexpensive to believe, which should have acted as a warning.

First the flight was delayed several hours, during which some of our fellow passengers dipped into the duty-free whiskey. By the time we boarded, several people were so drunk they weren't allowed on the airplane.

The pilot managed to get the rickety craft off the ground and up to the requisite thirty-five thousand feet. I dozed, which is my wont in a pressurized cabin, but the pounding feet of a stewardess, as they were called then, abruptly halted my sleep. She was dashing down the aisle toward the rear. In my ears was a high-pitched whistling sound. Coupled with the image of the world-record aisle dash by the stewardess, this formed an alarming scenario in my cranium. I wasn't the only one who was beginning to worry. A tangible unease had spread through the cabin. In an attempt to comfort his discomfited passengers, the pilot took to the intercom to announce that the rear door had sprung a leak. Nothing to worry about, though, he added. Just like having your car window open a tad on the freeway.

This information did nothing to relieve the tension.

Nevertheless, the plane rumbled on while the whistling from the broken door caused the folks in the immediate vicinity to cover their ears, to no avail. Again, Captain Comfort took to the airwaves. This time he informed us that we were going to have to return to Kennedy Airport. Our man in the cockpit performed a beautiful U-turn and dropped the plane to diving height over the Atlantic, and slowly we crabbed our way back to New York.

Back on the runway, we were apprised that another plane would be prepped for us, and asked to be patient. Several of our fellow passengers were too scared to continue with the bargain carrier and booked flights on Aer Lingus. Diana and self, however, were stuck, as we had no extra cash for such a luxury. So we waited. Eventually we were summoned to board the plane and get seated. All was done rapidly. As Diana and I buckled into our seats, a worrisome thought descended on me. *How do we know this is a different plane?* It certainly seemed familiar enough. I remembered then that I'd been reading a magazine in the other craft and had left the journal in the pocket of the seat in front of me. Sure enough, the mag was right where I'd left it. Several hours out, the whistling began again.

Down the aisle raced the stewardess, this time carrying newspapers under her arm. I arose and followed her back. The noise in the rear was unbearable, and those in proximity had fingers and napkins stuffed in their ears. Once more our intrepid skipper got on the blower, this time to inform us that we'd passed the point of no return, and it was Ireland or bust. Maybe not exactly those words, but something equally disquieting. Consternation reigned among the troops. Prayers to Jesus could be heard aloud. Appeals to Mother Mary too. Someone said something about praying to Saint Joseph, as he was a carpenter and might be able to help.

I began to think about the sea beneath us and what those waters held, the coffin ships that had brought the slaves and the Irish immigrants, the *Titanic*, submarines, the *Lusitania*, crashed airplanes, thousands and thousands of bones contributing calcium to the diet of the fish, who in turn nourished and supported thousands and thousands of fishermen on both sides of the Atlantic. The white woolen sweaters that the Irish fishermen wore are called Aran sweaters, and each has a pattern that belonged to a particular family. The oil in the wool stopped the salt water from rotting the pattern away even when the body it covered had decomposed, so identification of the drowned was easier. The sweater also absorbed water quickly, and the wet, thick wool would help sink the wearer, so drowning would not be prolonged. That fear of a slow death was the same reason that Irish fishermen of the North Sea would not learn to swim.

John Millington Synge's *Riders to the Sea* is one of the best one-act plays ever written. It's about fishermen drowning and how the women in their lives deal with the inevitable indifference of the sea. The eloquent words of grief and resignation would make a statue weep. Toward the play's end, the old woman who has lost all she loved to the sea raises her fist to the water. "They're all gone now. . . . There's nothing more the sea can do to me," she says triumphantly.

On the plane and out of my reverie, I stood and asked for quiet.

"There's nothing to worry about," I announced. "My mother will take care of things."

I had their attention.

"Would you like to meet her?" I asked.

Heads bobbed up and down in assent, so I removed the tin can from the overhead compartment and held it aloft.

"Here's what's left of her," I said.

"Oh Jaysus, Mother, and holy Saint Joseph! That's bad luck!" they wailed, as rosaries came out in force.

But soon after that the whistling subsided, and the captain announced the emergency was over. We landed safely in

Shannon. As we disembarked, my fellow passengers would not look in my direction. Had they, they would have no doubt noticed the smug expression affixed to the face.

------------

Frank converged with Diana and self on the tenth-century abbey and Mungret Cemetery, which is protected under the National Monuments Act, so it is illegal to cause any changes, stage any incursion, or perform any more burials there. Locked and barred gates held us at bay at first, but there was room at the gate top to get through. Frank climbed the gate, and I clasped my hands as a foothold for Diana and helped hoist her over. In a physical shape I am now quite envious of, over I went myself. We spread most of the ashes on the graves of her mother, her sister, Aggie, and her brothers, Tom and Pat. There was an aperture in the walls of the abbey that surrounded the cemetery within, and we placed most of the rest of the ashes there.

And that's where the remains remain.

# TEN

# The Father

*"I don't mind dying, the trouble is you feel so
bloody stiff the next day."*

GEORGE AXELROD

My first drunk was when I was eleven in Limerick. I was
with a pal from school named Jackie Adams. To me the pubs
of Limerick seemed warm, cozy, and inviting. Generally
speaking there were paneling of dark wood, dim electric
light usually coming from mini chandeliers, and mirrors with
discreet advertisements for Powers whiskey, Jameson whiskey,
Murphy's Irish Stout, or just Guinness, which was promoted
with a sign that read, "Guinness is good for you." It was a
statement nobody contradicted. There was always a slightly
acrid miasma emanating from these premises, molecules of
stout, whiskey, cigarette smoke, sweat, bad breath, and assorted
body odors drifting out to be sucked skyward, operated on,
and returned to earth for further application and recycling.

I got my first look inside a pub when I was six or seven.
During the Second World War, we children were dispatched

all over the town to get scarce cigarettes for the nicotine-addicted parents and relatives, and the pubs had signs over their doors that said "Licensed to serve spirits and tobacco." I'd make my foray beyond the front door, usually to be refused the cigarettes so desperately needed by the mother. I remember the pubs then as being quiet places with a few solitary men sitting or standing at the bar drinking glasses of dark liquid topped with a creamy white Roman collar of foam, each glass waiting to be quaffed and then refilled with just a nod toward the empty imperial pint. I was intoxicated by the quiet joy of these places before I even took my first sip of the forbidden stuff.

Jackie had lifted a pound from his older brother's savings stash, and in we went to Bowles Pub. We were two scruffy, scabby-kneed guttersnipes in short pants ordering two half pints of Bulmers cider. Why the barman served us I don't really know. It was a different time, of course, but even then getting children drunk was looked down upon. The two glasses of hard cider went past the lips and southward rather easily, so we ordered two more. Quickly tiring of the cider, we moved on to the harder stuff—Guinness stout. Up the Guinness was served, and down the Guinness went. From reading P. G. Wodehouse, I thought it appropriate to address a fellow in a service position as "my good man," which I did to the barman while ordering Adams and myself a refill. The barman must not have been a fan of Wodehouse, and didn't take the appellation kindly. "I'll give you my good man," he said. "I'll put my boot so far up your arse I'll be wearing you as a shoe." The statement was followed by an equally unfriendly request to leave his establishment. In short, I was thrown out of the first bar in which I drank.

Outside the pub we were a couple of legless drunks in short pants helpless with laughter at the memory of the barman's expression. At a local liquor vendor, we secured two little bottles of Powers, Irish whiskey in handy two-ounce servings. Down to the Shannon we staggered to sit and sip and watch the sun set peacefully beyond the glinting waters. I dozed off, or passed out, take your pick, and found myself ascending to mystical heights, communing with a different god from the terrifying, vengeful one that the ranting Redemptorist missionaries warned me about. I was in the company of a friendly, smiling, compassionate being who had levitated me above a world filled with sickness, misery, and poverty. We looked down together, God and I, bestowing blessings and forgiveness on everyone.

When I awakened I was alone. It had started to rain, my trousers were wet with piss, and I had a pain in my head that made me feel as if someone had hit me with a hammer. It would be years before I drank again, and yet I always remembered the experience and the spirit that had lifted me out of my miserable life. What I conveniently forgot, however, is that this benevolent spirit dropped me right back into the misery, feeling worse than I had to begin with.

It was no accident that my spiritual journey that day on the bank of the Shannon was fueled by spirits, as many such odysseys are. Later on, when my drinking became habitual, I always hoped that my ascent on those illusory wings of alcohol would allow me to get in touch with the All-Powerful

God Guy again, but it never happened—no matter how much I drank, and drank and drank.

For thirty years in all. A period of hilarity, great sadness, and the occasional suicidal thought. In that time I tried them all: the wines, the sherries, the ports, the beers, the stouts, the porters, the Southern Comfort, the Galliano, the Pernod, the Kahlúa, the gins, the vodkas, the rums, the whiskeys, the Scotches, the Irish whiskeys, the bourbons, the cordials, the brandies, the cognacs, the Irish Mist, the Baileys Irish Cream, the poteen (Irish moonshine), the Southern moonshine, the martinis, the Manhattans, the Tom Collinses, the orange blossoms, the Harvey Wallbangers, the Bloody Marys, the straight ups, the shots, the on the rockses, with a twist or an olive, shaken or stirred, all went down the gullet, and most were taken under the guise of social interaction. There were also a significant number imbibed to forget, or taken out of anger, most of which was directed at the father. Drinking alcohol because you're mad at someone is like drinking poison and hoping the other person will die.

I gave up the drink for good in 1985, ending the three-decade-long alcoholic tornado that had torn through the lives of those I loved and in its wake left the strewn parts of broken promises, relationships, and a marriage. Getting sober left me raw with feelings that the booze had hidden from me.

Jimmy Breslin once said that the trouble with stopping drinking is that you're left with the person that started you drinking in the first place.

My maternal grandmother thoroughly disliked the father, as he was some class of foreigner, him being from the other Ireland, the North, and looking and behaving like a Protestant. The Irish poet Brendan Behan once asked a Protestant woman from the North what a Catholic looked like.

"You can always tell them by their wee button noses," she said.

If that was the true measure of them, you'd have been hard pressed to find a Catholic in the Limerick of my youth, what with all the bulbous proboscises that abounded, noses that grew in direct proportion to the number of Guinness stouts swilled.

Under those circumstances my father and his fairly large hooked beak should have fit right in with the RCs of Limerick.

The father was the quietest man in the whole world when he wasn't drinking. In fact, he disliked talking with any of our neighbors, not because he thought he was better than they, but because, without the social lubricant, personal interaction was one of the most painful things he could imagine.

In one little house across the lane from us lived Mrs. Downes. Like a lot of the poor women of Limerick she had perhaps two yellowed teeth in her mouth. It seemed that every time Father would put on his raincoat and prepare to go out she'd come out and stand at her door. She had some type of radar for such things. He would peek out the window. "She's out again," he'd say, and he'd begin pacing up and down. After a while he'd look out again and see her again, and he'd sit down and take off his cap. Then he would get up and put his cap back on, look out the window, see her, and it would start all over again.

Invariably he'd give up, and when he'd walk out the door, he would wince at her high-pitched, gummy tone.

"Helloooo," she'd always say to him.

He was never given to violent acts when sober. He would go through a whole elaborate routine when he was going to punish us. He would meticulously roll up the sleeve to the gainsey. He'd take off his jacket. Position us just right. Raise his hand, and then tap us on the forearm with a couple of fingers. The blow wouldn't have frightened a flea.

But when he got the drink in him, it was time to head for the hills. He saved up all he had to say for when he was drinking. It was then all the slights against him, all the grudges he carried in his wounded heart, would come up and fly from him like great billows of fire. He became a towering madman ranting against those traitors who'd betrayed Ireland, and the British and Irish governments who neglected the men who'd fought for Irish independence. And though the cause of the rage in my father was always very clear, he was random in who bore the brunt of his wrath, except he did not hit the mother or us.

There was one incident when my mother sent me for a half pound of butter down to Toomey's shop. I was seven or eight at the time, and when I got to Toomey I completely forgot what the mother had sent me for. I said to Toomey, "My mother wants a half pound of sugar." So he ladled out the sugar, which was stored loose at the time and measured that way. I took the sugar back to the mother.

"I told you to get butter," she said to me. She sent me back, but Toomey, who was a cranky old fucker, wouldn't take it back.

"If you don't know what you want don't be coming in here," he said.

And so that was that.

Then, about five months later, the father got temporary work and as usual went off to dispose of his first week's wages at the pub and to give voice to his list of domestic, national, and foreign injustices. When he arrived home, he did so roaring drunk and singing.

Fill up once more, we'll drink a toast
To comrades far away
No nation upon earth can boast
Of braver hearts than they;
And though they sleep in dungeons deep
Or flee, outlawed and banned;
We love these yet, we can't forget
The felons of our land.

In boyhood's bloom and manhood's pride
Foredoomed by alien laws
Some on the scaffold proudly died
For holy Ireland's cause.

And brothers, say, shall we today
Unmoved, like cowards stand
Whilst traitors shame, and foes defame
The felons of our land?

Some in the convict's dreary cell,
Have found a living tomb,
And some unseen, unfriended, fell
Within the dungeon's gloom.
Yet what care we, although it be
Trod by a ruffian band—
God bless the clay where rest today
The felons of our land.

Let cowards sneer and tyrants frown
O! little do we care—
A felon's cap's the noblest crown
An Irish head can wear.
And every Gael in Innisfail
(Who scorn the serf's vile brand)
From Lee to Boyne would gladly join
The felons of our land.

When the last of the rebel's words came roaring out, he grabbed me by the hand. "Come with me," he said, and we marched down to Toomey's.

Inside the shop he banged the counter until Toomey emerged from some dark place, and the ranting, raving, leaping lunatic that once was the father confronted him.

"People didn't die for Irish freedom only to be left with sugar they didn't want and without the butter that they did!"

Toomey didn't know whether to scratch his head or run for the door.

"You and your sort are a disgrace to the human race in general and specifically Ireland!" the father bellowed. "You should be fucking ashamed of yourself."

Toomey couldn't cut the half pound of butter fast enough. And just to be sure, he followed the butter with bacon, sausages, and potatoes, desperately trying to assuage the volcanic eruption of this madman in his shop.

On the way home, carrying a bag of groceries, the father sang the Famine Song:

Oh, the praties they grow small, over here
Oh, the praties they grow small
And way up in Donegal
We eat them skins and all, over here, over here
We eat them skins and all, over here.

Oh, I wish that we were geese, night and morn,
Oh, I wish that we were geese
Till the hour of our release
When we'd live and die in peace, stuffing corn,
    stuffing corn
When we'd live and die in peace, stuffing corn.

Oh, they'll grind us into dust, over here
Oh, they'll grind us into dust,

But the Lord in whom we trust
Will return us crumb for crust, over here, over here
Will return us crumb for crust, over here.

But back in the slum house, I watched as the courage and bravado in the father faded like the dust in his song. With the drunk nearly gone, he skulked into bed to hide from the emerging shame. In the bunk he stayed for days, weathering the mother's rage at him. Of course, the temporary job went, as did the groceries, and we were back to our diet of bread, tea, and fresh air.

————

When sober the father had an unshakable faith and belief in the teachings and rituals of the Church. He insisted that the whole family go to Saint Joseph's for Mass every Sunday. He'd make us scrub our ears and noses, and wear the best of what we had, which wasn't much. Then he'd march down the lane with us following like ducklings. At bedtime we'd kneel and say the rosary. All five decades. All the Our Fathers. All the Glory Bes. And, of course, all the Hail Marys with the monks swimming.

We all belonged to the Archconfraternity of the Holy Family, said to be the largest confraternity in the world. Every Monday, Tuesday, and Wednesday, about two thousand Limerick men would gather at the church, where a Redemptorist priest would deliver a fire-and-brimstone sermon followed by devotions, prayers, and the singing of hymns. The church sold candles with a piece of paper around them so you wouldn't burn yourself from the wax. With two thousand fervent Catholic men, only men, holding lit candles in the church, the priest would shout:

"Do you renounce the devil and all his works and wiles?"

"We do!!!" they shouted back, as they raised their hands with the candle. Hot wax flew all over suits and backs of necks. Swearing and pushing ensued.

One night I remember the priest asking the crowd if they renounced the devil, and a man yelled:

"We do...the dirty fucker!"

When Father was drinking, God's love went out the window, and so did his love of his family. Given the choice of drinking the pay or bringing it home for food and clothing for us, more times than not the drink won.

―――――――――

"There's a place for everything and everything in its place." I must have heard him say that a million times. The great irony was, he was hardly ever in the place he should have been, and that was home with us.

He went to England, where there was a severe shortage of manpower in the factories turning out weaponry and supplies for the English troops battling the Germans. Consequently, tens of thousands of Irishmen migrated from the Emerald Isle to work and get a wage the likes of which had never been seen in the home country. Millions of pounds winged their way by wire to neutral Ireland's impoverished families, catapulting them into an imitation of the middle class. The McCourt family was an exception to this munificence, as our loving daddy took his wages and himself to the nearest public house and left them on the bar, thereby improving the local economy and leaving his own family in dire want. On Saturdays all the families with daddies in England arose so that the children could watch out for the telegram boy bearing the piece of paper printed with pounds, shillings, and pence. Yelps of glee were to be heard as the mothers opened the little envelopes and then dashed to the post office to cash the wire. This was soon followed by the aroma of Irish bacon and sausages wafting its way into the Limerick air. There were times when the telegram boy rewarded us with our own wire, but that was a rare occurrence. My father did write short letters on occasion, exhorting us to obey the mother, our teachers, and our priests, and to say our prayers, attend Mass, and in general be good boys. Nothing about shoes or food or rent. You could say he was a spiritual man not given to materialistic concerns.

Never did he utter the word *love*, and though the song "The Felons of Our Land" does include the word, it does so in a general and abstract way, one not as intimate and embarrassing as telling your spouse or children that you loved them.

Was I angry at him? Of course. I drank for years trying to quell the rage I felt at what he'd done to us, to me—or, more important, what he hadn't done for me.

————

My own alcoholic bottom, as they call it, came during a trip to Limerick in 1985. Frank and I went there to perform

*Blaguards.* I drank with a furious abandon. It felt as though it had all been flung back into my face: the shame of our existence in that city, the relief money we were always on, the begging at the Society of Saint Vincent de Paul for a bag of turf, the hypocrisy of the Holy Mother Church. It was a wonder I didn't drink myself into the grave. And for what? Nearly all of those who were the target of my anger were dead or gone.

When I came back from Limerick, having almost drunk myself to death, I did so beaten, defeated, broken, disheartened, and depressed. Frightened by my depression, I went to my doctor, who said the problem was I was eating, smoking, and drinking too much.

"So what are you going to give me?" said I.

"A bill if you don't get out of here," he remarked. "You know what to do."

I said no to alcohol at frequent intervals over the term of my drinking life, but alcohol wouldn't take no for an answer. When my friend Walter was in a serious physical condition and his physician told him that heavy smoking and an addiction to alcohol were the causes of his illness, he replied, "Thank God; I thought you were going to say it was my fault." Alcoholism can be a fountain of laughter and cause waves of merriment whilst going unobtrusively about the business of murdering those of us who need to drink.

The sensations-feelings-thoughts that accompany the ingestion of the booze all seem real, all seem logical, and all seem reasonable, during a drinking life, and whatever the mission or project suggested by the booze-addled mind, it has to be started and completed right away. Sometimes these missions are harmless, like my late-night calls to Rollie, but sometimes they can involve a little matter of suicide. One friend of mine found himself perched on the Williamsburg Bridge not knowing how he'd gotten there. Luckily for him, he came to his senses just before he might have taken the dive. Other acquaintances who almost recovered from their alcoholism slipped back to drinking and did not slip back to life. Hanging by rope, poisoning by pills, and jumping from heights did them in. One friend got to drinking around Christmastime, got in the car, and drove into the Adirondack woods. He was able to climb from the wrecked vehicle but began walking deeper into the forest. After some time he got tired and lay down to nap. He never awoke. Instead he froze to death. By all appearances his life had been in perfect condition. He was very successful in business and had been married for many years, and had several accomplished adult children. But alcoholism is a sneaky foe and does not tolerate happiness.

Even when it's not propelling one to an early ending, untreated alcoholism will settle for a later death. Brothers Mike and Alphie both had their battles with the booze. Alphie did stop drinking but was a secret smoker, which might have contributed to his early death. Brother Mike also gave up the booze but did not get completely sober, as he liked the other weed.

The only one of the brothers who sidestepped the addiction was Frank, who could always have his daily glass of vino or two without deleterious aftereffects. His two romantic catastrophes did involve alcohol-related incidents, but I'm certain it was his perceived love that drove him to such lengths and not the booze.

Taking a portion of my doctor's advice, and in absolute denial about my drinking problem, I set out to trim the diet. I attended a twelve-step meeting for overeaters, which used the same tenets as the more famous twelve-step meetings for alcoholics. In fact, they didn't even have their version of the twelve steps, and instead suggested that you substitute the word *food* for *alcohol*. It was then that I realized I was only fooling myself. My primary problem was that I drank too much.

As it happened, around the same time, I had gone to California seeking to scale the studio walls in search of acting employment. Though I got the occasional gig, those walls seemed to grow higher, and the entrances stayed locked to me. One day led to the next, a dreary and seemingly endless succession in which hope inexorably diminished. I was miles away from my love, Diana, the children, and my brothers.

When I first heard the words *Alcoholics Anonymous*, I thought it meant drinking under an assumed name. In those twelve-step meetings, they tell you it's the first drink that gets you drunk. Armed with this information, I went out to my local establishment and ordered two shots of Irish whiskey and, as hawks do, watched as my man poured them and placed them in front of me. I moved the first shot he poured aside and happily threw the second one down the gullet. The next thing I knew it was morning and I was in a strange apartment alone in bed with my head banging like a bass drum in a marching band.

Of course, I had no idea that, for an alcoholic, the first drink starts an obsession that leads to compulsive drinking.

In California I began to stick my head into the sobriety meetings, leaving unimpressed with the stories of grief over lost jobs, failed love affairs, and dead cats. Yes, there were plenty of redemptive tales filled with alcoholic adventures, and those piqued my interest. But the truth of it was that I had one foot out the door, ready to resume my drinking life.

Until, that is, at one meeting a speaker who was introduced as Jimmy strode to the front of the room. Jimmy's face had more creases than a dried riverbed, and his mouth was filled with teeth that looked like little tombstones in an abandoned grave-yard. He also had two cauliflower ears that seemed to move independently of one another when he spoke. There was no doubt he was a Noo Yorker, as he talked from the side of his mouth and still somehow achieved the volume of a foghorn. His message was quite clear. He was an ex-convict who had been locked up for a total of eighteen years in various jails at various times for various offenses mostly involving burglary and theft. One of his more successful operations had involved dressing in overalls, stealing a van, and, with a confederate in tow, entering funeral homes, where he'd proceed to remove the furniture and rugs from the waiting rooms. He would act very officious and wave a clipboard if anyone questioned him. "We're bringing in all new stuff," he would say. On the occasion that someone became suspicious, he and said confederate would run for the door. But all that was behind him now. He was sober and drug-free and helping other addicts and alkies.

Though I found Jimmy entertaining, I ran right into a

roadblock when he began to talk about God and the divine intervention he said God had worked in his life. Immediately I began to conjure justifications for my escape. No one can be more of a snob than a former slum dweller, and I began to tell myself that I had nothing in common with this low-class criminal. Still, somehow I knew that if I walked out the door, I might never come back.

After the meeting I approached Jimmy and asked him if he would consider being my sober sponsor.

"I knew you were going to ax me," he growled.

"And how's that?" I asked.

"Because I know you, and God has a sense of humor."

The baffled look on my face begged for an explanation. Jimmy complied.

"Do you remember Election Day 1959?"

"Why would I need to remember that?" I asked.

"Come on, now; something happened to you that day."

I pulled open the door to my memory bank. It wasn't easy, rusted as it was from all the booze. In 1959 I was still a partner in Malachy's and, because of an old set of rules called "blue laws," the saloon was closed during polling hours. And then it came back to me. When I opened the bar after the polls closed, I found the drawer had been pulled from the register and several of the locked cabinets jimmied open. We'd been heisted.

As the memory showed in my expression, the cemetery in Jimmy's mouth spread into a wide smile.

"You?" I asked.

Your man answered with a nod.

I pointed out to him that one of the twelve steps suggests that the recovering alcoholic make amends to those he's harmed in the past.

"My amends to you will be being your sponsor and helping you get sober," he said, to which he added, "There was practically nothin' in the register anyway."

And so, accompanied by my burglar sponsor, off I stepped on a journey that returned my life to me.

But not all at once.

In fact, life seemed to get worse before it got better. The career was a struggle. I had ended a long association with the daytime drama *Ryan's Hope* the year before and desperately missed the steady income. Over the course of my acting career, I've had parts in some forty movies. There was a dearth of them at this time, however. Yes, my relationships improved, and Diana was delighted. "You make more sense," she said. But the pall that had descended upon my cranium in Limerick had not dissipated. I missed my friend the bottle and all the conviviality of my drinking life. Of course, my memory had selectively forgotten the morning hangovers, the shameful behavior, and the selfishness. Instead I imagined myself in a smoking jacket holding a brandy snifter and dispensing witty remarks to a coterie of attractive and fabulous friends. Although kneeling in front of a porcelain altar would have been closer to the truth, alcohol called to me.

I didn't experience a God moment in my early sobriety as many of those who populated the meetings said they had. There was no bounding or leaping with joy. Trudging would be a better way to describe those early days of not drinking.

No white light or divine sign appeared to me. Instead, mine was a slow turn away from the darkness.

Still, I didn't give up.

When I came back to New York, I started going to meetings all over Manhattan. Good orderly direction solved the issue I had with the God component of the twelve-step program of recovery. The hoop to a sober life was big enough for an atheist to jump through. Diana and I began to do yoga and even started to bring groups of like-minded friends up to the apartment. We loved to camp and hike. In sobriety I embraced these excursions in earnest. We traveled to Nova Scotia and Vermont with packed tents and gear. In the forest I realized that the higher power so often talked about in meetings surrounded me. We hiked mountains and swam in streams. With each breath of crisp air, with each star-filled night, with each step holding my love's hand, the thought of alcohol receded further and further until it was nonexistent.

Where once I'd searched for liquid wings to help me fly, I found that the ground under my feet was where the real spiritual journey took place.

The walk wasn't pleasant all the time. In early sobriety, when the frosty crust of alcoholism began to crack and fall away, the hot molten feelings beneath began to bubble up to the surface. I was both raw and vulnerable. I felt there were scores yet to settle.

In his old age the father had settled down in Belfast, where all his material needs were taken care of: housing, food, medical, and home help, all provided by the government of the country he had fought against when he was in the old IRA, and denounced and railed against in stories, poetry, and songs.

I wrote him in my early sobriety. I was in my late fifties, but I felt like a wounded schoolboy as my pen flashed across the page. All the rage, the polluted tide of anger, came spilling out of me. The attack on him was full frontal and comprehensive. I began with the death of my sister, Margaret Mary, and the twins. How could he not provide enough basic sustenance and shelter to keep them alive? I wrote of the hunger and cold and skin diseases we suffered from malnutrition. I railed against his hypocritical preaching on religious duties. Where was his blessed Jesus when we were starving and dying in the filth he allowed? And, finally, when I was nearly exhausted, the thought of perhaps his worst transgression against me flew into my mind.

---

In a period of intense piety at the age of eleven or twelve, I began thinking of becoming a priest. I looked at those guys garbed in black and with their stiff white Roman collars, respected on Sundays bedecked in colorful robes, hectoring, lecturing from the pulpit, the power of God oozing from them as they told us how to live.

So when the mantle of piety floated down and enveloped me, and the thought that I might become a priest lodged firmly in the chest, I mentioned it to the scoutmaster, who suggested I might have a chat with a priest who was home from the missions in Africa and was staying at his sister's house. To say it was unusual for a slum kid like me to reach the rarefied air that was the holy orders is an understatement.

First of all, as we had nothing, we gave little to the Church, so why would the Church spend money to board and feed me while it taught me the ways of the priesthood? And there was also the common thought that being poor was a form of punishment, that somewhere along the line someone must have pissed God off for him to have given us the life he did.

Undeterred by the long odds, I followed my calling and off I went to the fancy house where Father Quinn was staying. We sat in big wooden chairs that had comfy cushions. After a few perfunctory questions about why I was interested in the priesthood, His Reverence stood and began pacing back and forth in front of me and speaking in an intense monotone about the dangers of giving in to impure thoughts. I was eleven, and was what today would be called a "late bloomer." I don't think I'd had even my first inkling of a thought about sex. I certainly hadn't discovered the joy of masturbation yet. So I was totally confused as to what His Reverence was talking about. When he stopped pacing, bent down, and unbuttoned my fly, I didn't know what to do or where to look. He told me that he had to see if I would become erect. He said that chastity was a most important part of being a priest, and temptation abounded, and sinful women would want to fondle me. The arousal needed to be beaten from me, he said. I don't know if I knew what an erection was, but I wasn't about to get one. I sat there petrified as his cold hand held my penis.

Finally he told me to button my fly. He said that the discussion we'd had was the same as confession and that I wasn't to tell anyone about it. I managed to say something about becoming a priest. "Your family can't afford it," he said. "There's schooling involved."

I walked home with a building shame that had no escape because there was nowhere for it to go. There was no father with arms open to run to, no father's lap to cry on.

Father Quinn wasn't the only one. There was another priest. And a pious prick who was the head of the Legion of Mary in Limerick, a statue eater, as Angela called them, for their penchant for kissing the marble sculptures of the saints in church.

And with these too I kept the secret to myself while my father drank in the bars.

Why had he allowed his child to suffer the ultimate indignity without a father there to protect him?

I finished my long screed. Checked his address on Glen Road in Belfast. Attached the postage. And off the letter went. In my imagination I saw a tear-soaked letter back from him with humbled words begging for forgiveness.

Two weeks later, what I got was my own letter back to me with a handwritten notification on the unopened envelope.

"Gone away," it read.

How fucking appropriate.

No, I said to myself. He's not going to get away with it that easily. The old fucker wasn't going to die before his derelictions and desertions were flung in his hypocritical face. I hied myself down to the post office, where I found a bigger envelope, onto which I affixed a registered mail label. Again I wrote down his address and handed the letter to the postman behind the window.

Back home, I waited.

And then the response came.

The note was brief, but in his unmistakable Victorian copperplate handwriting.

*Dear Boldy,*

*I received your most welcome letter and I understand how you must feel about things. I will write you a longer letter soon as I am rushing to catch the last post.*

*Yours sincerely,*
*Your father.*

Once again I began to feel the rage well up within me. I hadn't seen or talked to him in over thirty years and he sent me a couple of dozen words as if he lived across the street from me.

I sat with that anger for a couple of days and chewed on it as a starving man rips into an old, leathered chop. I wondered during those maddening days if the rage toward him would ever subside.

And then Frank called with the news.

The father had died in Belfast.

What next happened I couldn't have imagined. What was sniffle at first steadily grew to a heaving sob. I wept for Margaret Mary and the twins. I wept for little Alphie and Mike. I cried for Frank. And then I cried for me until I expelled the last of the tears I had.

And then it was done. The anger at him was gone, as if the tears had carried it out of my soul.

---

The first letter I sent to him was sent back by a caregiver. The father was in the hospital, and she took it upon herself to return all correspondence for him to the sender, for what reason I have no idea.

I don't know whether he was suffering some illness when he sent the note. Perhaps that was the reason for the brevity of it. And yet the missive was exactly the length it should have been.

During that emotional time, the image of him in Limerick came to me. Malachy McCourt Sr. was a slight man with expressive brown eyes that became lit when he told his imaginative stories. His Northern Ireland accent and his whimsical sense of humor brought those stories alive. I remember being six or seven and sitting with Frank and the babies Mike and Alphie near the dying peat fire in the house on Roden Lane. He would spin out of thin air a tale that included all the characters from the Lane: Mrs. Downes and Toomey and Paddy Reidy and his *Limerick Leaders*. But he set it in an exotic port or the deepest jungle or some fabulous city, and his words would transport us there. He was better than any show or movie.

I held his note again in my hand. He blamed its brevity on wanting to make the last post. In the British military, "the last post" is the equivalent of taps in the United States Armed Forces. My father was handy with words, and perhaps the phrase was his way of cleverly telling me he was going to die. In any case, the words that he wrote were just enough to release a lifetime of hard feelings.

When all was said and done, he was a drunk, just as I had been. And though I was more of a hail-fellow-well-met, bounding around the better-known saloons of Manhattan, than the abandoner he was, I too had put my need to drink in front of family and duty. I too had hurt and disappointed many of those close to me. Maybe not to the extent that he had, but in the same self-centered way nonetheless.

I left my first wife, Linda, and our two small children, Malachy and Siobhan, stuck in the apartment while I was out setting the night ablaze. There marital fidelity became a joke of sorts. Honesty disappeared, and this was followed by the inevitable lowering of standards; I found myself becoming the biggest liar in the USA. I couldn't meet the basic financial obligations like paying rent or utilities. I scrounged through the couch for change to get on a subway. I cheated my partners in business. I slunk home as the sun came up, with eyes as red as my beard and hair. And yet nothing made me angrier than when the wife or a brother pointed out the havoc being wreaked on my life by the drink.

"How dare you!" I said, indignantly. And out I would go on another drunk. I was fortunate that my liver held out, and that I wasn't beaten or killed, considering the places my drinking took me. I didn't care. When I was drinking I didn't care about anything or anyone but me and my next drink. Meanwhile my old pals shame and guilt nattered away in my ears, a cacophony of negativity. Shame reminded me I had never been any good, while guilt told me I was a fraud and that I would soon be found out.

It was perhaps in the realization of my own selfishness that the healing with my father began.

———————

Frank, on the other hand, never forgave the old man. Not being an alcoholic, the brother didn't have the same experience and insight that I did. "He knew what he was doing," Frank would spit when talking about the father. Frank and Alphie made the trip to Belfast for the funeral. Malachy Sr. had died in the Royal Victoria Hospital, and the corpus was kept in what is known in Irish hospitals as the death house, usually an unadorned stable-like building where bodies are washed, shaved, and made presentable for public scrutiny.

Frank told the story of kneeling on the prie-dieu beside the body on the gurney and gazing as reverently as he could at the old man's countenance. The false teeth were missing from the father's mouth, which collapsed the face in such a way that the hooked nose almost touched the chin. The sight reminded Frank of a deceased seagull, and that thought brought on an uncontrollable storm of hysterical laughter. The brother put his hands to his face to try to stem the hilarity but was unsuccessful. Behind him the other family members—cousins, nieces, and nephews—were gathered, and from that vantage Frank's shaking shoulder and snorting sounds were construed as indications of grief and sorrow.

Frank knelt there until he could gather himself, which took some time.

———————

The father lived until he was eighty-eight, outdistancing his wife and all his children, except, that is, for me, though at this writing I still have three more years to go to overtake him. He gave up the drink and tobacco quite a few years before he died, which no doubt helped in his longevity.

The one thing that I will never know is if he felt the least remorse for what he did to us.

If he did, he told no one about it. At his funeral, Frank and Alphie introduced themselves to the priest who had conducted the service, who had known my father.

"I didn't know Malachy had two sons in America," the priest said.

"He has four," Frank answered.

He also put enough aside to buy himself a plot and a headstone that cost him $1,100, someone said. When I heard the price I almost laughed. He hadn't provided so much as a pair of shoes for his sons, and yet for all eternity he'll lie under an extravagant marker as if he had been the lord of a castle.

The father is buried in the graveyard of a country church near Belfast that was exclusively Protestant until Catholics started dying in the area in large numbers. I've never seen his grave or headstone.

Having been a sober one for many years, I know that the

job of the parent is to guide, protect, and love the child. I know what it means for a child not to have someone to stand behind him as he looks out at the world.

There was only one time my father held that position for me.

For dinner, as we called lunch in Limerick, the school would serve us a half-pint bottle of milk and a bun. Frank wrote about the bun and how it was a prize if it contained a single raisin. The cleaning woman for the school served the lunch. She was not very clean herself. One day she handed me the little bottle of milk and a bun that was half the normal size. What's more, it was moldy. I was starving, but I wouldn't eat it. Instead I drank the milk and put the bun in my pocket.

At the time my father wasn't drinking. I came home from school that day and showed him what the cleaning lady had given me to eat. The next morning he put the bun in his pocket, took me by the hand, and walked me to school, where he marched us right into the headmaster's classroom.

My father stood straight, his eyes clear and hard. He took the bun out of his pocket and held it front of the headmaster.

"How could you expect the boy to eat this?" he said to the man. "It's disgraceful."

The headmaster agreed that it was wrong and later went down to tell the cleaning woman not to ever do it again.

I was never more proud of my father than on that day. He didn't ask me to die for Ireland, nor was he drunkenly tilting at some other windmill. He just wanted his son to be treated right. It was great—as small as it was.

And it was all I ever wanted from him.

# ELEVEN

# The Brother Frank

*Had I the heavens' embroidered cloths,*
*Enwrought with golden and silver light,*
*The blue and the dim and the dark cloths*
*Of night and light and the half-light,*
*I would spread the cloths under your feet:*
*But I, being poor, have only my dreams;*
*I have spread my dreams under your feet;*
*Tread softly because you tread on my dreams.*

    W. B. YEATS, "HE WISHES FOR THE
    CLOTHS OF HEAVEN"

Frank McCourt's last residence on earth, the Visiting Nurse Hospice on Second Avenue and Ninety-Sixth Street, New York City, was a comfortable place with a good-size bed and a living room with sliding doors leading onto a very pleasant terrace. Although at the very end his faculties were shutting down like lights in the theater—the eyes no longer reading or watching television, the ears no longer hearing, so no more witty responses—there was no evident pain. The hospice was a very human place and allowed visitors any hour of the day or night. It provided little handbooks about the process of dying itself and what happens from the actual moment a person dies, including algor mortis, which is the linear decrease in body temperature: two degrees Celsius in the first hour; one degree each hour after that. Taking a body's temperature is sometimes how forensic scientists approximate the time of death. We didn't need the scientists. We were there.

The brother's final journey began with a seemingly minor matter of a growth on his knee, which despite the urging of his wife Ellen he neglected. When he finally got around to having the growth looked at by a physician, it was, of course, the scourge of the fair-skinned Irish, melanoma. It had made its way into the groin lymph nodes. Then followed an experimental treatment that involved removing blood from his body, twenty vials at a time, sending it to California, where it was strained or something, sending it back, and reintroducing it into his body. By this stage he was in the hospital after collapsing in Tahiti. Frank never tired of traveling the world and giving his sometimes outrageous talks and wry observations, and sharing his absolute delight in the attention paid his groundbreaking memoir, all the time bolstered by the love of his beautiful pal and spouse Ellen, who never lost her sense of humor.

The onset of the melanoma-induced meningitis shattered any hope. None of us wanted to admit that it was now a matter of weeks before Frank would die.

Frank was quite conscious for much of that time before he lapsed into what seemed to be a coma. But there is no such thing as a coma, they're just dozing, they're conscious and aware. Though they can't respond verbally because of the so-called coma, the dying will understand any bit of business you have out with them. Better then to say your piece under those conditions than to have them die without having cleared your conscience.

Frank didn't have much of any narcotics, and he kept a good sense of humor. My sister-in-law Lynn, brother Alphie's wife, is disabled and uses canes, so her entrance is very noisy. One day she arrived at the hospice and came clunking into the room, and Frank by this time had lost his hearing, but his sight was still there. "It was very quiet in here until you arrived," he said with his usual deadpan delivery, which got Lynn and me laughing hysterically.

I suppose it's normal, during events like watching a loved one slowly die, to go back over one's relationship with that person. There were moments during those last weeks of Frank's life when I thought back to decades before all the fame and regard had descended on my brother, and wondered how it all worked out the way it had. For years the brother trudged his way through an educator's life, toting thousands of pieces of paper, correcting, marking, and forgetting, anonymously teaching, being known as Malachy McCourt's brother, with no time to write his story. His was a life that could have easily gone by in the way that most do, known only to a limited circle of family and friends, a coffin closed on the pile of what-ifs and might-have-beens, and a small paid obit in the local rag.

That, as you might know, was not the case with Frank McCourt.

Although *Angela's Ashes* was an international bestseller, a Pulitzer Prize winner, and thoroughly beloved throughout the literate world, there were those who, out of begrudgery, an Irish blend of envy and spite, sought to tear down Frank's beautiful writing with accusations of fabrication. Life in the lanes of Limerick, they said, was not nearly as bad as Frank portrayed it. As an eyewitness, I can attest to the horrid conditions. I'm also Frank's brother and as such perhaps not the most unbiased voice. But most of those who disputed the events in the lives of the McCourts of Limerick weren't there or alive at the time, or had some other agenda. One particularly nasty local radio host who seemed to dedicate most of his airtime to attacking Frank had written two memoirs of his own Limerick childhood, both of which sank like stones.

If you have Irish Alzheimer's, the old joke goes, you forget everything but the grudges. Frank laughed at those who hated him. He saw that they were powerless and helpless in the face of the worldwide identification with *Angela's Ashes*. As President Bill Clinton said when he spoke at my brother's memorial, "Frank told everyone's story through his own."

I'm too old now to give those yahoos and naysayers who sought to pull my brother down any more of my brainpower than I already have. They're more to be pitied than censured. Besides, what can get lost in all the rancor is the inherent goodness of the people of Limerick, a city that has a history of decency and generosity. Frank was the first to extol the virtues of many of our neighbors in the lanes: the Downeses, the Knights, the Sextons, the Harans, the Meehans, and above all that magnificent royal family, the Horrigans, who would never see any man, woman, or child go hungry. All of them faced what we faced and did so with dignity and a goodness that, considering the circumstances, was miraculous. Not every Catholic in Limerick was Christian, but so many of them, particularly those with little of the world's material goods, were charitable. It's easy to give when you have enough to give. Giving is quite another thing, however, when what you give is all you have. For the most part, Laners suffered nobly and complained in great style, with a poetic attention paid to language. Frank knew this and celebrated it in *Angela's Ashes*.

———

Sigmund Freud once said that the Irish are the only race impervious to psychotherapy. Old Freudy would have had a field day trying to crack the nut that was the brother Frank. How much of his miserable childhood—the absent, drunken father, the depressed and distant mother, the deaths of three of his siblings, the uncaring government, the punishing and dismissive Catholic Church, and the abject poverty—he carried into his adult life can be guessed at but not measured. To be sure, though, Frank had his demons.

One of the remembrances I had during that time of his

dying was of the night in 1959 when he came into Malachy's and said he was going to kill himself. He had come in to say good-bye. Of course, I asked the inane but necessary question, "Why?" Apparently he'd had a row with the girlfriend at the time, a woman known to me, and my other brothers, as the War Department. She'd gone off and married some misfortunate, and Frank couldn't go on living.

The relationship had been tumultuous, to say the least. For one thing, he was having trouble writing when she was around. The atmosphere was always loud, often angry, and certainly not supportive. I always imagined her screaming, "Nobody would be interested in your piece-of-shit, slum-dwelling childhood," or something equally eloquent. I figured she would insist that her own family's story would be infinitely more interesting, as she was a descendant of New England whalers and had aristocratic blood and so forth. Apparently one of her ancestors had been on a whaling ship that sank, leaving those who survived in a lifeboat. Oddly, given that they had been on a whaling ship, they weren't able to catch fish. So they drew lots to see who would be killed to provide sustenance for the rest. The cabin boy drew the short straw. Though this was unlucky for him, the crew was fortunate to have someone so fresh and tender to eat. They survived, and years later the War Department's ancestor was asked if he knew the cabin boy.

"Know him?" he said. "I ate him!"

The moral of the story is, never marry a descendant of man-eaters, or you could end up the main dish.

When I asked Frank how he proposed to kill himself, he

said he was going to throw himself into the East River. I then asked him if it would be all right to walk him to his final destination, as I didn't think he should go leaping into the river fully clothed with cash and identification in his pockets. The walk was leisurely enough, a ten-minute stroll from the saloon, taken up with a conversation about his last wishes. Outside of books and a small bank account, there wasn't much of an estate, but it's the same bother as with a large one. I brought up the fact that Frank was a reasonably good swimmer, and good swimmers, generally speaking, tend to keep the head above water. Just jumping into the water doesn't guarantee instant death. When we approached the riverbank, one intemperate remark of mine nearly caused him to take the leap. "Why would you kill yourself for a bitch who is at this moment spreading her legs for another guy?" As the novels say, an anguished cry from his lips rent the air. I had to physically restrain him from taking the last leap.

My strategy, as it were, was to discuss at length all his reasons for committing suicide. As previously stated, Jews have the monopoly on guilt, Catholics (particularly the Irish) have the monopoly on remorse, and Protestants have regrets only. I tried to inculcate Frank with some shame about suicide, going to hell for that unforgivable sin, and how delighted and satisfied and gratified the War Department would be if the low-class Irishman had killed himself for her.

After a couple of hours of disconnected subjects I suggested to Frank that he come back to the bar. There we could drink until closing time at 4:00 a.m. and go for breakfast and thus, being nicely warmed by booze and nourished by food, he could go energetically and gently into that good night—if one is trying to procrastinate someone out of killing himself, 'tis best to include death in the list.

The final act of the episode was that the War Department dumped her first husband, and, much to the brother's misfortune, she married Frank and got back to the bloodletting. The brother once said that the Irish are the only people who commit matrimony.

————

For years afterward the brothers—Mike, Alphie, and I—wondered why Frank suffered the torture of this union. And yet he stayed on. There was, of course, his daughter, Maggie, and that was the reason for staying. He told me that he could never go to the lavatory and have a peaceful bowel movement, so he suffered constant constipation. No shit! The result was that the man got colon cancer and still stuck with her.

I did not relish the role of war correspondent, so it was not a surprise that during this time I lost contact with the brother. It would be many a year before he walked out the door of the War Department.

In the meantime Frank continued teaching at Stuyvesant High School and living in relative obscurity as I lit the New York night ablaze.

Frank was a wine drinker, and not the drunk that I was. He never understood the concept of alcoholism as a disease. Of the father he said, "He knew what he was doing."

After his departure from the War Department, we resumed

speaking nearly every day on the phone, a practice that would last until the end of my brother's life. I guess one would consider ours a close relationship, except for the undeniable fact that we're Irish and as such went no deeper emotionally than was needed.

———————

For Frank there was another relationship that ended swiftly and amicably, followed by another relationship that was punctuated by violence and anger. This woman was connected to a drug dealer who physically attacked Frank on the street outside the old Stuyvesant High School in Manhattan, Fifteenth Street to be exact. Soon after, I got the call from the brother that he was again going to end it all, as the love of his life had decided that being a drug dealer's mistress was preferable to being attached to a schoolteacher.

At that time Frank was sharing an apartment in Brooklyn Heights with a painter named Jonk Kling, who could copy just about any classic work of art and sell same. The apartment was in the building over a bar where Jonk spent a great deal of his time. I went to the bar and asked Jonk for the key but didn't tell him the purpose of my visit. Up the stairs I went into the rather dingy, run-down bachelors' quarters. There was no sign of the brother until I pushed open the bathroom door. There, in a bathtub filled with bloody water, he lay with his eyes closed. There were a couple of empty bottles of wine on the floor next to him. He had cut his wrists with a knife that wasn't very sharp—the damage looked more serious than it was. I got him out of the tub and found some adhesives and wrapped his wrists. I sat with him until eight o'clock in the morning, until I was sure he was asleep and OK. The next morning I called him, and he told me he was fine. Once more it was a tale of being abandoned by a blonde WASP of limited intelligence, this one the moll of a drug-dealing thug, and once again he didn't know how he could go on living without her.

––––––––––

Now, it is a well-known fact that writers are more likely to commit suicide than normal people. In fact, there is a recent survey in one of those psychology journals, and no doubt a reputable rag, that says scribes are twice as likely to pull down their own shade, as it were. Writers dead by their own hands fill bookshelves. Virginia Woolf stuffed the pockets of her overcoat with stones and jumped into a river, Spalding Gray dove off the Staten Island Ferry and drowned, Ernest Hemingway toed the trigger of a shotgun pointed at his head, and Hunter S. Thompson used his fingers on a .45. Sylvia Plath did what was once called "the Dutch act," putting her head in an oven and turning on the gas; John Kennedy Toole ran a hose from the exhaust pipe into his car and closed the windows. Toole died thinking himself a failure. It was only after his death that his *Confederacy of Dunces* won the Pulitzer Prize. The list goes on. And that's not counting the ones who drank themselves to death, which, by conservative estimate, is a number that exceeds the population of Ohio. Depression, drink, and broken hearts: you name it, and writers die from it. Very few, however, go from natural causes. The same passion that fills the page with words that burst with emotion fills their heads with self-murderous frustration.

But what about those who end their lives before they fill pages? It's said that in November of 1953, after ingesting a prescription medication, Dylan Thomas downed eighteen shots of Irish whiskey in the White Horse Tavern, then staggered home to the Hotel Chelsea, where he collapsed and was shuffled off to Saint Vincent's hospital, where he died a few days later. The author of "Do not go gentle into that good night" was thirty-nine, and died with a thousand unwritten poems.

And what of those writers whose careers have not even begun?

Perhaps Frank's attempts were more drama than substance. But if I hadn't come over that night to Brooklyn, the water might have had gone crimson instead of light pink, and then the world would have never known the talent he possessed.

And I wouldn't have had the beautiful brother I had for the next thirty years.

Thankfully, the bro would come to his senses and decide that blondes were too dangerous, and so kept his eyes open for a brunette.

There must have been a dearth of them in the circles that Frank traveled. He was fifty-nine and in the Lion's Head when one walked in the door. Ellen, thirty-five, single, was there with a girlfriend. Frank, twice married, retired schoolteacher, was there with a drink and his pals. He and Ellen left the bar and went out for falafel and came back in love.

It was Ellen's encouragement that made its way through the ear canal and into Frank's cranium. And so he began to write in earnest.

Meanwhile a few writers and actors—Terry Moran, Sean Carberry, Pat Mulligan, and I—had been meeting for lunch every first Friday of the month, and we began to call ourselves the First Friday Club. In those initial years, Frank couldn't come because he was teaching. When he retired from the classroom, he decided to give us a try.

The series of events that led to *Angela's Ashes* began with a conversation with the novelist Mary Breasted Smyth at the First Friday Club. The exchange went something like this:

**MBS:** What are you up to, Frank?

FM: Ah, not much, you know.

**MBS:** Doing any writing?

FM: Fooling around with a little autobiographical thing.

**MBS:** Can I see it?

FM: Sure.

Though not exactly the repartee of the Algonquin Round Table, it got the job done. Mary saw Frank's "fooling around" and thought it was marvelous and asked Frank if she could take it to her agent. Of course, this wouldn't be any story at all if it went right from there to publication, fortune, and fame. So Mary Smyth's agent dismissed the manuscript out of hand. "Irish books, especially ones by new writers," he said, "don't sell." But Mary believed in the work and knew another agent, this one the mother of a babysitter who used to work for her. At first the babysitter's mother, Molly Friedrich, wasn't interested either. But Mary asked her to read just five pages. That was all it took. She asked Mary how to get in touch with Frank.

Molly Friedrich then sent the first chapter to Nan Graham, the famous editor at Scribner.

I knew none of this at the time. I knew Frank was writing a book. But I didn't know about the agents or the publisher or any of the other business. I found out only when Frank called to tell me that they'd offered him $125,000.

"Fantastic," I said. "Congratulations!"

When I hung up the phone, I started crying tears of joy for my brother who had struggled so long and so hard. I cried for me too. He had won, you see, for us, his brothers, too.

I read *Angela's Ashes* only when Frank sent me a copy, and did so all in one shot. Though the story was a family story, Frank never thought it necessary to ask his brothers for permission to write about us, using our names, our experiences, our physical characteristics, our personalities, our sayings, our songs, our lives without our say-so. The mother and father were dead, and if they were alive, they would not have given their consent for any story of their lives.

But I was very impressed with the details. The brother got them all right according to my memory. I thought he was too gentle in places that I would have been more savage, particularly when the book concerned Laman.

When I put the book down, I concurred with what Jimmy Breslin had said—I thought it would win the Pulitzer Prize. Jimmy and I weren't the only ones. The book had what they call "buzz."

The *New York Times*, however, at least in its first review of the book, did not concur. The guy who wrote it was a professor at NYU whose father was in the Royal Ulster Constabulary. He had published a memoir that sank, so maybe it was a case of sour grapes, an emotion not uncommon for a particular type of Northern Irish. In the end it didn't matter. The first *Times* review was a dog paddle against the tidal wave of praise that would follow.

I was proud of Frank and his accomplishment. But those fans of Frank would tell me how much *Angela's Ashes* had affected them, and how tough and touching it was, and how they still wondered how Frank could have survived it all. Forgotten was the fact that I'd lived the same life, endured the same conditions, watched the same brothers and sister die, experienced the same hunger, same cold, same schools, and same absent father. The only difference was that I did not nearly die of typhoid fever. I would tell them I was going to write my tome and name it *I Read Your Brother's Book* because I heard that phrase so many times.

But *Angela's Ashes* pulled open the door to a room where my brothers and I had hidden with our secrets and shame. Out into the sunshine we climbed and told our stories. And none of it would have happened without brother Frank and his memoir.

A year or so after the book had come out, I heard there was an *Angela's Ashes* tour in Limerick. I happened to be in Dublin doing PR for a movie I'd done, so I hopped down to Limerick and found out where the tour started from the Irish

tourist board. When I arrived, I saw a group of people standing around.

"What is going on here?" I asked.

A tourist with a strong German accent said, "*Ze Angela's
Ashes*. Very interesting."

I was wearing sunglasses and a cap.

Then Michael McDonald, the little guy running the tour,
spoke: "OK, ladies and gentlemen, the tour will start in about
ten minutes and will last for about two hours, and I can't
guarantee anything except it will rain about fifteen minutes
into it."

Just before we started, the little fellow came up to me.

"Would you remove the spectacles?" he asked.

I did.

"Ach," he said. "I knew it. Malachy McCooort." That's
how they say it in Limerick. "Now, what am I going to do?"

"Whatchu mean?" I asked.

"Ah Jesus, what if I get it wrong?"

"I'm not going to correct you," I said.

"Can I tell them who you are?"

"Oh God, don't do that."

So off we went, and it did rain, and he didn't tell them
who I was.

————

It's unlikely that I would have had much success in publishing
myself if Frank had not cleared the way and opened the golden

door. Indeed, it was a friend of Frank's who got me working on *A Monk Swimming*, a highly intellectual laddie named Charlie Defanti. Here is an example of how a simple answering of the telephone, and a few words, can change your life.

Phone rings:

"McCourt here."

"Hi, Malachy, Charlie Defanti, listen." I do. "I've been thinking you have a book in you too, just like Frank's."

Me: "A book in me? How do I get it out? Have a literary bowel movement?"

Charlie: "I'm serious. I've heard your wild tales, and I have a friend, John Weber, who is a small publisher, and he will give you an advance and guarantee your getting published."

And that's how my literary career began, and after a series of negotiations, acquisitions, and auctions conducted by an agent named David Chalfont, a Hyperion publishing editor named Maureen O'Brien offered a healthy advance, and did so without my having written one single stitch. It's a wonder the publishing business has lasted as long as it has.

When I began to turn in chapters of *A Monk Swimming* (the name came from a childhood memory of mangling a line in the Hail Mary, "Blessed art thou amongst women"), Maureen would call me bubbling with enthusiasm. "This is marvelous," she enthused. "Everyone in the office is reading, and they all can't wait for what's next."

The praise mystified me. All I was doing was thinking of stories that had happened to me and writing them down. I didn't realize there was any art to that at all.

*A Monk Swimming* did not disappoint. I hit the *New York*

*Times* best-seller list at number three, and overnight I was a published author with contracts fluttering in the windows from as far away as Spain and Australia. A couple of reviews said I was no Frank McCourt, which was not news to me, as I had been convinced from an early age that I was Malachy McCourt. The begrudgers said I was raised aloft, flying by holding on to my brother's coattails. I saw Frank often in a tuxedo but never in tails. Still, as Dorothy Parker once said, the two loveliest words in the English language are *check enclosed*, and there were plenty of those lovely envelopes at the time.

One regret, however, was that I never ascertained what my beloved brother thought of my literary efforts. I had eight books published, and Frank never said a single word about any of them to me, and, to this day, I do not know if he ever read a word I wrote. I often wonder if I should have risked asking him what he thought. Yes, I did think about it.

I didn't have nearly the formal education Frank had. After graduating from NYU, the brother got his master's degree in teaching from Brooklyn College. He later went to Dublin to start on his doctorate. He didn't need such an advanced degree; he knew more about the English language and how to form it into a story than anyone who would have tried to teach it to him.

Of course, after all his schooling, all those years that he taught writing, and all his own writing that came before *Angela's Ashes*, I'm sure he was a little pissed off that I just waltzed in, picked up a pencil, wrote down all the loony stuff I remembered, and found myself on the best-seller list.

But there was no animosity, at least of which I knew. And

although Frank never talked about my writing, there was never a shortage of things to discuss. There were family and friends, and years of memories to exhume and inspect and then drop back into their holes in the ground. And there were laughs.

One time driving us to New Hope, Pennsylvania, where we were going to perform our play, *A Couple of Blaguards*. It was after Saint Pat's Day, a wintry day, and the busy interstate route we were traveling had started to freeze over. The side of an eighteen-wheeler loomed like the *Titanic* in front of us. My knuckles were white on the steering wheel.

I slammed the brakes, and the car went sideways into a skid.

"Hold on," I said to Frank.

"To what?" he responded in a perfect deadpan.

I wrecked the car, and Frank ruined his shoulder and spent the night in the hospital, but there was another story, another laugh.

My brother Frank was my best friend, and he was so from the day I was born. And though we never talked about my writing, Frank was a writing teacher to me just as surely as he was to the thousands of high school students who sat in his classroom over all those years. If not for my brother Frank, I would have never had the courage to put my words on the page, nor experienced the joy and tears that come with it.

———————

So it was a very sunny Sunday the nineteenth of July, 2009, and the family, Ellen, brother Alphie, Lynn, Diana, Vickie, a friend, and I were playing some sort of word game when we heard a faint gurgling sound from the bedroom and a concerned rapid deployment brought all to the bedside (me following in my electric scooter, still incapacitated from a broken leg) to witness Frank expelling that last breath and lapsing into that stillness peculiar to the newly dead.

It was exactly three minutes past 3:00 p.m.

The clock still dispensed minutes, and the July sun still shone on the terrace, and the planes flew over New York City, and the traffic still moved on Second Avenue. The nurse came in with a stethoscope at the ready and gave us the final, final word. He's gone! Pulled the blanket over his face and summoned the undertaker. Although he was being cremated, Ellen said the necessary official stuff was best handled by a licensed funeral home. Three men and a gurney arrived, the men put Frank's body on it and covered it with the blanket, not a body bag, and off they went, and Alphie suggested we sing "Now Is the Hour" as the little procession exited.

Now is the hour
When we must say good-bye,
Soon you'll be sailing,
Far across the sea.

Which is as far as we got in the song due to the outburst of sobbing and cascades of tears, and that was the last glimpse we had of the vibrant, witty, iconic man of many words before the crematorium reduced him to ashes.

Then came the after-death accolades and two lengthy

obituaries in the *New York Times*, and papers in Moscow, China, and Australia carried the news, and my phone rang and rang with condolences, and the mail brought hundreds of "thoughts and prayers," as they say. One phone call was from President Bill Clinton, who asked to come to the sort of wake we had at Rosie O'Grady's on Seventh Avenue, New York City, conducted by Ted Smyth, husband of Mary Breasted Smyth.

Then we had a big memorial concert at Symphony Space courtesy of our friend Isaiah Sheffer, now deceased.

Peter Quinn did the MC duty with wit and dignity, the brothers Alphie, Mike, and self did our rendition of "Barefoot Days," the composer David Amram spoke and played, and fellow Limerick man Mick Maloney led his Washington Square Harp and Shamrock Orchestra. It was all grand, and Frank would have approved.

In looking back on his life, I think Frank understood everything about men, but he understood not one thing about women, and the same applied to finances. He did have the gift of laughter and a great sense of irony. He was oddly generous, oddly frugal—he mentioned none of his brothers in his will—and certainly was no saint, as some family members can attest to. A saint is a severely edited sinner, and Frank was far too intelligent to be a saint, so instead he was an original sinner. All in all, he was a far better man than most at achieving the good and not so successful at being a lesser human being.

It is redundant to say he was a marvelous writer. And though there were rough patches, as they say, and some unresolved issues, he was a good brother, an amazing teacher, and a good friend, uncle, father, husband, and grandfather.

I don't know what happens after death, nor does anyone else, despite the bullshit we are told, but for now the spirit of Frank McCourt is with us.

I am glad he was born. I'm glad he lived. I'm glad he wrote. I'm glad he was my brother. And I'm sad that he died.

In *A Grief Observed*, C. S. Lewis reminds us that our mourning does the dead wrong. "They beg us to stop," he wrote.

There were long moments after Frank's death, after all the reminiscence and tears stopped, when I felt empty, sorry for myself and about the loss that I had experienced, and not the one that Frank had. Mourning solely concerns us, the living, and is selfish in its way. Frank lived a magnificent life, a wondrous life, and it's better to leave it there and not wallow in what I miss.

# TWELVE

# And the Dead Arose and Appeared unto Many

*Cast a cold Eye*
*On Life, on Death.*
*Horseman, pass by!*

EPITAPH OF W. B. YEATS,

DRUMCLIFF, COUNTY SLIGO

There are a few so-called bad words in the English language that I don't like, but *fuck* is not one of them. To my mind there are many other words far more threatening and villainous. Not too long ago, I heard a young father admonishing his son for using the off-color gerund by saying that he "hated" that word and that he would "kill" the boy if he heard him say it again. Now, I doubt the father literally hated his son or meant to end his life, but the word *hate* is much more bloody awful than the featherweight word he scorned. So for all you people who admonish the featherweight word *fuck* and embrace the bloody awful ones like *hate* and *kill*, I have three words for you:

Go fuck yourself.

Another word I don't particularly care for is *sibling*. It always sounded to me as if the person were speaking from on high when they used that particular designation, and that the people whom they labeled as such were inferior beings or hated enemies, as in *sibling rivalry*. Better to use the good old *brothers* and *sisters*, in my opinion. Makes them more human, which in some cases they are.

To refresh the memory, Angela and Malachy Sr. mothered and fathered seven children, one little girl and six boys, all sister and brothers, and not one sibling among us. In order of appearance, the children were Frank; Malachy Jr., who is myself; the twins, Eugene and Oliver; and Margaret Mary, all born in Brooklyn, USA; then Michael and, finally, Alphonsus, called Alphie, born and reared in the slum of Limerick.

It was Margaret Mary's death in infancy that caused the mental breakdown in the mother, Angela, and gave the father, Malachy Sr., the excuse to spend his time and money in the local pubs. Then, with the generosity of neighbors, friends, and relatives, the parents and four surviving children embarked for Ireland, where it was hoped the mother would recover her equanimity and reenter reality and perhaps the father would stop relying on the alcohol to assuage his grief.

But in Ireland it was not long before the dark mantle of death was laid on our household. Eugene and Oliver, the lively, funny, delightful little lads, took sick and died within six months of each other. But then it was as if the big God Guy upstairs decided that the McCourts had suffered enough death and needed the light of life that comes with the cry of newborns placed by angels under a cabbage leaf for the mother and father to find.

————————

Brother Michael John was actually born in the maternity muni hospital called the Lying-In Hospital. The mother was whisked there on February 24, 1936, where she gave birth to a perfect-looking little boy. The baby grew even, white teeth like the Americans and smiled easily with friendly eyes. There was a musical quality to his voice.

As per usual for us slum dwellers, Mikey John left school at fourteen and got survival employment at the Savoy Cinema restaurant, which just so happened to be right next to the Lying-In Hospital. After the mother moved in with her drunken lout lover, Laman, Frank and I moved out to live with our uncle, Ab Sheehan, who would be characterized as developmentally disabled in modern jargon. We found out in later years that Laman had frequently used our brother Mike as a punching bag. That had left very deep scars not only on the body but forever in the mind of the brother.

Still, throughout his life, Mike had a penchant for singing and seemingly learned songs by osmosis. If he liked a tune, the tune became his. My father had made the brother Frank and self sing patriotic songs about dying for Ireland but got the Irish divorce early in Mikey John's life, so the young lad was free to sing all the non-Irish songs he wanted to his heart's content. At one point he discovered Al Jolson in the barrooms of Limerick, and he became a leading practitioner of all things Jolson, particularly that tuneful "The Anniversary Song." But "My Mammy," "Sonny Boy," "April Showers," and "Swanee" were all part of his routine. He didn't use blackface because shoe polish cost money and was too difficult to wash off, but Mikey John was a welcome addition to any party.

As he had for mine, Frank paid Mike's way to the USA and New York, where he worked for me in Malachy's on Third Avenue. A series of other saloon jobs would follow, leading him all the way to LA, where he found work in a celebrity joint called Chez Joey. Never one for fawning over anyone, Michael was like a harbor lighthouse in a storm for the well known. No less than John Wayne, Montgomery Clift, Kirk Douglas, Burt Lancaster, and John Ford sailed into Mike's bar to be imaginatively disrespected and imaginatively insulted by the master of invective. One story has it that the proprietor, Joey, had given Neil Armstrong a peanut to secrete on his person and return from the moon with, so it could be displayed in the saloon. Armstrong did as requested and the peanut was encased in a glass container for all to see. One night brother Mike popped open the glass container, cracked open the shell, and ate the peanut. He placed a non–outer space peanut in the glass case, where it was admired for years.

In 1969 a man named Perry Butler decided to open a New York–style saloon in San Francisco and realized that the place could not function unless it had the quintessential New York–style wisecracking Irish bartender. So, two years removed from the Summer of Love, and without any flowers in his hair, off Mike went to San Fran. While the counterculture of hippies gathered in Haight-Ashbury, Mike established himself behind the bar in San Francisco. In the minds of the media there he became the foremost commentator on all subjects dear to saloon frequenters, especially those of which he had little knowledge. In a way, bartenders are like hairdressers: the best of them have big followings. Mike's flock contained worshippers of all stripes, including dockworkers, cops, firefighters, politicians, musicians, advertising executives, lawyers, whores, and conservatives, at the risk of being redundant. (Here's a joke Mike told about barristers: Why are lawyers' graves dug twenty feet deep and not six? Because deep down they're good people.) Mike's style of tending the bar was particularly appealing to writers and newspaper scribes, including a Pulitzer Prize–winning one who worked for the *San Francisco Chronicle*; the columnist Herb Caen was known as the "voice and conscience" of the City by the Bay. But in moments of dire need, as deadlines approached, it was Mike who would provide some pithy witticism to rescue the column and columnist. Caen repaid the brother by being a faithful follower and with tips in money that folded.

———

Mike's calling was working behind the stick, as the jargon of saloons goes, dispensing drinks, wisdom, wisecracks, and observations, such as on the day two marines entered the premises and ordered two glasses of wine.

"The flag at Iwo Jima was not raised by chardonnay drinkers," Mike opined.

"Forget the wine," the marines answered. "Give us two Irish whiskeys."

He disliked what he called "cork sniffers." One man, in an effort to be a wine expert, had Mike standing and waiting for him to order.

"I'm thinking of something somewhat windy and a trifle smoky," he said.

"Do you want a drink?" Mike asked. "Or to start a fire?"

He didn't particularly enjoy insulting nobodies, as he felt nobodies, especially self-important nobodies, should be left in ignorant misery. Anyway, an insult from Mike made a nobody an instant somebody.

Though working at the bar was Mike's vocation, his children were his life, and they included a passel of temporary tax deductions: Mary and Angie from his first marriage, who are bright and loving daughters; Mikey John, a young man of infinite jest, as they say, who will no doubt be a gift to the written and spoken world; and Katie, also a shining mind, both of whom are products of the loving marriage he had with his second wife, Joan. His love extended bountifully, of course, to his granddaughter, Mary, and her husband Rick's delightful Sophie.

It would be a series of physical incidents that finally felled this pillar of the lush life. First he fell on one of those famous San Francisco trolleys and fractured his leg. Then came the diagnosis of prostate cancer, the treatment for which caused a mild heart attack. He was next laid low by pneumonia, and then dementia arrived, and so to bed and so he was dead.

During his life, San Francisco's news media gave the

brother the star treatment. "We have one real celebrity in San Francisco, his name is Michael McCourt," shouted one article about him. Another called him "the Holy Grail" of barmen. In his book on North Beach, Ernie Beyl told of Mike's encyclopedic grasp of old movies, actors, football picks, and legendary drinkers. When his bartending days were finished, the owners of Original Joe's quickly and without fanfare employed Mike just to sit at the bar and chat with customers. He had served and delighted three generations of San Franciscans and dispensed the rite of passage in the form of a first drink to many of his beloved followers. In death too the city's media paid appropriate homage. The headline in the *Chronicle*'s story about Mike's death read "Bartender of Renown Dies."

Brother Alphie and my son Conor went out to San Fran to represent the family at the various celebrations and memorials, which were hugely attended and at which numerous knowns and unknowns stood to relate their favorite Mike story, quip, or yarn. Writers and columnists in San Francisco and beyond are still quoting his witticisms.

The McCourt love of the word coursed through Michael's veins and yet, even after the success of the brothers' books, he had no desire to write one himself. When one interviewer asked him why not write about his childhood in Limerick, he responded, "If I do, I will write of the difficulty we had in hiring decent help, of the decline in the quality of watercress sandwiches, of the trouble we had keeping our palm trees trimmed and the shamefully low price we received from selling our polo ponies." He also said he would write his memoir when all the other brothers were dead. But he wouldn't be the last to go.

Mike left his heart in San Francisco, as the famous song goes, and took a piece of mine when he died on September 5, 2015.

Less than a year later, death would strike again.

On June 26, 2016, Frank's publisher, Scribner, invited family and friends to New York's Sheen Center to celebrate the twentieth anniversary of the publication of *Angela's Ashes*. I've never been against a good bash, but I didn't see the purpose of celebrating the fact that two of the brothers were gone and the two remaining twenty years older. Still, it was a joyful evening hosted by Professor Joseph O'Connor, who occupies the Frank McCourt chair at the University of Limerick, Ireland. Among the lights that shone on the stage that night were Gabriel Byrne; the former poet laureate of the United States Billy Collins; and the Pulitzer Prize–winning Irish poet Paul Muldoon. Brother Alphie was in top form, speaking eloquently and poetically about Frank.

The event was a rousing success, and at its conclusion, Alphie and I said our good-byes and promised to talk during the week, which was customary. As I did with all my brothers, we talked on the phone often. Alphie was waiting on the delivery of two very important parcels, the first of which was a check. It seemed that brother Alphie and I were in a state of perpetual abeyance when it came to receiving money in the mail. This particular check was for an appearance we had both made at a chain bookstore. He was also hoping to receive a parking permit for people with disabilities to make life in New York City a little easier for him and his wife, Lynn.

That Friday evening I arrived home and checked the answering device for messages, and there was the voice of Alphie in a somewhat stentorian preaching intonation imitative of one of those Redemptorist fathers of our youth, announcing without preamble, "'And the dead arose and appeared unto many.'"

Paraphrased a bit, the words come from a story in the New Testament, which, by the way, is about two thousand years old. Anyway, the tale concerns one Joseph of Arimathea, who was nice enough to rent his tomb to Jesus for a three-day weekend. To the deal he also threw in a large stone for privacy against looters and apostles. According to the story, the rock was no match for the earthquake in Jerusalem, the first and only seismic event ever recorded in that part of the world. The quake, it was said, snapped the stone like a Ritz Cracker. It was then that an angel appeared all dressed in white and told Mary Magdalene and Mother Mary that Jesus had arisen and they could find him in Galilee. At the same time, this earthquake had opened up not only Jesus's tomb but also the graves of some of the dead buried in Jerusalem. A whole lot of people who had died suddenly got up out of the holes in the ground and started visiting their families, many of whom had already turned their relatives' rooms into man caves and guest rooms. It was an unlikely event, to say the least, which is why Alphie used the line to let me know he'd received the check.

It was also his way of saying good-bye.

_____

It was an unusually pleasant and clear summer day in late July of 1941 that Alphie arrived on this earth. The day was remembered by Frank and me and to a certain extent Mike, who was five at the time, because we had not been allowed to leave "Italy," as Frank called the one warm room upstairs in our slum house. The downstairs was being used for something, but we didn't know quite what. That it was the process of a birth was the furthest thing from our minds. We all knew that babies were found under cabbages, left there by angels, and there was no cabbage growing in our kitchen, which we knew for certain.

In any event, the father stood guard at the top of the stairs as strange, high-pitched groans and screams from the mother wafted up to us. Those sounds were accompanied by the voice of Nurse O'Halloran, the midwife, saying to the mother, "Push, good, breathe!" As the groans got louder and the nurse's voice got louder, all Frank and I could surmise was that there was a tug-of-war contest or some other game being played downstairs. Then all of a sudden, there came a squall of cries and laughter. The father made a dash and nearly tumbled down the stairs, followed by Frank, tiny little brother Mike, and me. And there we beheld the mother smiling at a little red-faced squawking baby. The fact that there wasn't an angel or a cabbage patch in sight did not diminish the good and pervasive feeling one bit. You could count the number of moments of pure joy in our life in the Lanes on a left foot, and this was one of them. Plus we didn't give a fiddler's fart about where the baby came from, as it was now noon and summer outside in Limerick cad we had a great need to be released to play, which, because of the high spirits of the parents, we were.

Our tyrannical maternal grandmother had a special devotion to a saint with the moniker Alphonsus Liguori who founded the Congregation of the Most Holy Redeemer, aka the Redemptorists. The headquarters of these terrorists, known for their hellfire-and-damnation sermons, was located just a stone's throw from our house across O'Connell Street in Mount St. Alphonsus Church. There wasn't an optimist in the lot. And so Alphie was named after the saint and henceforth suffered the arseholes who thought they were so original and so witty when they yowled the first line of that song: "What's it all about, Alfie?" Of course, the different spelling didn't matter to these Einsteins. My own experience has legions of people who insist on calling me Malachi, which rhymes with *eye*. Malachi is Old Testament, I tell them, and although I used to drink with some of those guys—and Malachi means "messenger from God," not all that bad a designation—my name is Malachy, which rhymes with *knee*, which I promise to place in the bollocks of those who call me Malachi.

There are others who think I've never heard the word *malarkey* before. They will break into hysterical laughter while trying to say, "You know...hee...hee...hee...what they...har... har...har...should have...hee...hee...hee...called you?" I will, of course, pretend I don't know what's coming. "No," I say, "what should they have called me?" Then comes the burst of laughter at their own wit: "Malarkey! Har...har...har..." My response is always, "Did you think that up all by yourself?"

When they nod, I say, "Wonderful, let me add your name to the 7,847 other arseholes who have said the same thing before you."

————

Not only was Alphie born on a beautiful day, he would continue to bring the sunshine into the slum dwelling on Roden Lane. In his own memoir, a beautiful, lyrical read called *A Long Stone's Throw*, Alphie told of one of his first childhood memories. Once in a while, Frank and I were given charge of our youngest brother. We took him out in his pram and one of us, usually Frank, stood at the top of Barrack Hill while one of us, usually me, waited at the bottom. Frank gave the carriage a shove and Alphie came flying down the hill in our own version of Coney Island's Cyclone roller coaster. Now, it was generally my job to catch the carriage. This one day, however, I was distracted by something, and Alphie whizzed right by me and across Wolfe Tone Street and right into the open door of Leniston's Pub.

It was a prophetic moment, although it would be a long time for the prophecy to be realized.

Alphie was the only one of the McCourt boys who attended secondary school, which was taught by Christian Brothers in Limerick, and that included Frank, who was accepted into New York University only after devising some creative paperwork. Like Frank and me, Alphie joined the Scouts at an early age, where he learned to play the bagpipes, an instrument that the Irish gave to the Scots, who haven't gotten the joke yet. When Alphie reached his early teens, Sean Costelloe, our neighbor, recruited him into Sinn Féin, the nationalist organization. During the 1950s the popularity of the IRA began to surge again, a tide that culminated, perhaps, on New Year's Day in 1956. It was then that my old friend Seán South led an IRA raid on a police barracks in Northern Ireland.

The raid, ostensibly to procure arms for the struggle, was bollixed from the start. The mines they'd set to blow the doors off the barracks were duds, and the truck carrying the column of fourteen IRA Volunteers pulled up to the wrong house. Seán and his partner, Fergal O'Hanlon, a sixteen-year-old kid, were shot as they tried to plant the mines, and four of the Volunteers from the truck were also shot and wounded. According to official British Conservative authorities, Seán was dead when Her Majesty's representatives arrived, and they produced his bullet-riddled body to prove he had resisted to the end. His comrades told a different tale, however. They said he was alive and was shot to death as he lay there gravely injured.

Seán South was executed without jury or trial.

The population of Limerick at the time was forty-five thousand, and Seán South's funeral drew fifty thousand.

In Seán South's honor, our neighbor Sean Costelloe wrote the Irish republican ballad "Seán South of Garryowen." Though Seán South wasn't from the section of Limerick known as Garryowen, the song, first performed by the Wolfe Tones, is world famous, used as stirring background music in many Hollywood movies, and still sung by countless Irishmen in bars.

Although he barely knew our father, the same nationalism embodied by him and our grandfather flowed through Alphie's physical veins. That Ireland had been occupied for over eight hundred years by decree of Pope Adrian IV, that it had been given to King Henry II, for which the papacy had gotten one penny per annum per habitation, was quite enough for my patriotic brother Alphonsus J. McCourt. He set out to do his best to liberate that occupied part of Ireland from conservative British rule.

Alphie was nonviolent; the cumann was a political club. But he did his part in the struggles by selling the *United Irishman*, a newspaper that represents the republican movement in Ireland. He hawked them on O'Connell Street by shouting: "Buy the *United Irishman*. Help yourself to freedom!"

———————

In 1959 Alphie came to New York with the mother for a visit. After a few months he applied for a green card with plans to stay (the mother had already made that decision). There was a waiting period for the alien registration card to become official, during which time it was forbidden to leave the country. I was playing rugby then, and we had a match in Montreal. Alphie, who had played a few times with us, wanted to come.

"They will never know" was his sound reasoning for disregarding the governmental rules.

They knew.

He finally made it back to New York, as a resident of Canada on a visit, about a year later.

For a few months he lived with my first wife and me, then he took a furnished room on the West Side of Manhattan, and finally he settled in a small apartment in the Bronx. There he worked as an elevator operator and for the Burns Detective Agency, guarding factories at night. He also enrolled at Lehman College.

Following Frank's and my path, he enlisted in the army and spent a good part of his enlistment in Chicago inspecting food in the slaughterhouses, and in Norfolk, Virginia, with about two hundred thousand sailors.

In 1966 the army gave Alphie the honorable good-bye. (For some reason, probably because of his distaste for bureaucracy, Alphie didn't become a citizen of the United States until he was in his seventies. He served this country in the armed forces, swore allegiance when he joined, just didn't want to stand in line for the country. When he finally did, he was truly proud.)

———————

He took an apartment on Lexington Avenue across from the 92nd Street Y and made good on the prophecy of the pram rolling into the pub by taking a job tending bar in a saloon on Second Avenue. Alphie was softer than the rest of the McCourts, more sensitive, perhaps because he lived alone with the mother in Limerick for the longest. But he got into the New York swing pretty quickly and started dating a few young women from the East Side.

A lifelong career behind the bar, however, wasn't his plan.

His namesake, the saint, studied law before he found his true calling, and Alphie had a yearning to learn the law himself. Back to Ireland he went, where he enrolled in University College Dublin. There he read law, as they say in Ireland, his tuition paid courtesy of the GI Bill, as it's known in America. His barrister dreams, however, lasted only a short time, at the end of which he set out to find himself and what he really wanted to do.

When Frank found out that Alphie was absent from Dublin, he tracked the youngest brother down to California and elicited this cryptic explanation from Alphie: "I went to California because the constant rain in Dublin depressed me and I couldn't stop dreaming of California sunshine."

Who could blame him?

And for a while it seemed brother Alphie would settle into a higher existence as a California hippie. But after a year of Ravi Shankar, magic mushrooms, and hash, it was back to New York, where he once more got himself involved in that most addictive occupation, one that has no future and even fewer prospects and produces a forgettable past while engaging you in depressing daily contact with people looking for a life out of nothingness while tumbling into an abyss of nowhere. In other words, he went back into the pub business.

He also began seriously dating one of the younger women he met during his first sojourn to the big city. Lynn was a nice Jewish girl from Long Island who said that she'd set out to find and marry a guy with an Irish brogue. When Alphie would explain that theirs was a short-term relationship and that he was heading back to California as soon as he could

223

get a bit of a stake together, Lynn would nod and smile and then go out and buy a new set of dishes or silverware for the apartment they shared. Soon Alphie realized his California dream was no match for *bashert*, the Yiddish word for destiny. In a nondenominational church, a Catholic priest performed a Jewish ceremony, both Lynn and Alphie stepped on a glass, and under the eyes of every imaginable deity they were pronounced man and wife.

They held the reception at their apartment, where a hundred of us or so ate Irish saloon food and danced to the music from a rented jukebox.

Not too long after the nuptials took place, Lynn and Alphie's one and only child, Allison, was born. It was around that time, I think, that the adventurous Alphie went into partnership with a couple of Hispanic folks and opened up a Mexican restaurant named Los Panchos on West Seventy-First in Manhattan. To say it was an enormous success would come under the heading of understatement, but not at first. This was 1977, and the restaurant struggled along for months, teetering on the precipice of failure. The food was authentic, and the location wasn't bad—near Lincoln Center with its philharmonic, ballet, and opera—and the management was cordial. Having spent many years in the business myself, I have always found it mysterious that some places that run without imagination thrive, while others that have seemingly everything going for them wither and die. In those early months at Los Panchos, the latter seemed to be the case. The register rarely rang.

One aspect of the restaurant that did show some early

popularity, however, was the small patio where customers could dine alfresco, as my Italian friends might say. It was the patio that would turn the tide of the tacos. That summer New York City was thrust into darkness from a blackout. That era in New York was not particularly conducive to a lightless experience. During the blackout, looting in the poorer sections of the Bronx and Harlem was rampant, as were the fires that consumed the slums. This was the summer of the Son of Sam murders. That fall, while announcing the World Series, Howard Cosell would utter the famous line, "The Bronx is burning." Afraid that the lawlessness would find its way south to white Manhattan, most of the restaurant owners on the Upper West Side shuttered their doors during the blackout. There were no lights or refrigeration anyway, so why bother? But brother Alphie saw an opportunity. One of the great things about the great city of New York is the camaraderie its inhabitants exhibit during calamity. The candles placed on the patio tables of Los Panchos drew the air-conditioningless hordes like the proverbial moths to the flame. Cold food and warm beer flowed until the wee morning hours, and from that moment on, the Irishman with the Mexican restaurant was known to many, and Los Panchos as your neighborhood joint.

Alphie was on the map.

At home, Lynn developed spinal problems that affected her mobility. Ultimately the condition worsened to the point that she required braces and canes to walk. There were problems with daughter Allison too. A developmental disability meant constant care.

Though Los Panchos soared for years and years, and Alphie was the most financially successful of the McCourt brothers, in time things there too began to falter. Conflicts among Alphie's partners arose, and in a burst of optimism the brother opened a somewhat fancy joint in an unfancy neighborhood on the West Side of Manhattan. It was near the Fashion Institute of Technology and would have done well had he catered to students with simple fare like hamburgers and sandwiches, but the decor of tablecloths, flickering candles, and dim lighting only exaggerated the absence of customers. After the restaurant closed, practically broke, with a physically handicapped wife and a child with a severe mental handicap, Alphie went looking for work. He found a job supervising the installation of kitchens and bathrooms in a limited-income apartment complex. He would keep that job for most of the rest of his working life.

Like his father and brothers before him, Alphie had once been a bit cuckoo with the drink but had the good sense to give it up. Being a loving, caring, and unselfish father and husband to Lynn and Allison took up the space where the booze had once roamed.

Alphie could be a peculiar sort. Frank and I would chortle about the unusual things that annoyed our youngest brother. One was the habit people have of opening the lid of a public mailbox after depositing a letter, to make sure it went down.

"Why do people do that?" Alphie would wonder.

"Why do you care?" we'd ask him.

"Well, it annoys me," he'd say.

Why that amused Frank and me, I have no explanation for. Another of Alphie's observations had to do with possessive pronouns and how they change during the course of a day. "In the morning," he'd say, "it's *I* get out of *my* bed and get into *my* shower, have *my* coffee, say good morning to *my* wife and *my* children, take the bus to *my* office, where I greet *my* boss and later have *my* lunch. Then, after lunch, for some reason, it's *that* arsehole boss, *this* stupid job, *that* damn ride home, *your* troublesome children, *this* inedible dinner, *that* goddamn wife."

It was this awareness of language that imbued Alphie with the tools of a poet. He loved to read and write verse. Here's one:

Brother Malachy now has a book of his own
Brother Mike from California rejoices by phone
Brother Frank as we know is a Pulitzer winner
And they can, if they like, have twelve eggs for their
  dinner.

It wasn't a big surprise that Alphie would write his own memoir. *Publishers Weekly* called *A Long Stone's Throw* "a nomadic adventure worthy of Ulysses." Brother Frank heaped praise on Alphie's book and did so from a place of both love and admiration.

———

And then it was the end of June 2016, and Frank's publisher, Scribner, decided to celebrate the publication of *Angela's Ashes*. When the night came to its inevitable conclusion, I stood onstage with Alphie and my teenage granddaughter Gillian, where we sang "Barefoot Days."

One week later Alphie was on my voice mail.

"And the dead arose and appeared unto many."

His recorded voice said, "I have to go and lie down now."

There is that strange prayer that terrorizes children, you know the one: "Now I lay me down to sleep, I give my soul to God to keep, and if I die before I wake, I give my soul to God to take."

Alphie did die before he woke. I'm quite sure that he hadn't been thinking of handing his soul to anyone or anything at that moment.

The next thing I remember of that day is Lynn on the phone sobbing. She had gone in to wake him from his nap.

"He didn't move," she said. "His body was cold."

My son Conor happened to be in the neighborhood and got there very quickly. As a recently retired member of the New York Police Department, he was able to get the local precinct to come and certify that there had been no foul play. He also arranged for the local undertaker to come and remove Alphie's body. A neighbor who is a physician certified that the cause of death had been a heart attack.

Alphie had been a couple of days short of reaching seventy-five years, and outside of deafness in one ear had been in good health. He was the one the rest of us looked to. Not only did he take care of his two disabled dependents, wife Lynn and daughter Allison, he hoisted me whenever I called on him.

This odd-mannered poet, this talented, literary, caring husband, father, brother, uncle, lay down to take a nap and didn't wake up. A very short time thereafter, his six-foot mass of bone, brain, tissue, muscles, ligaments, hair, nails, skin, kidneys, lungs, liver, teeth, genitals was reduced to a small residue of ashes that was placed in front of a blown-up photograph at the front of a funeral room filled with folding chairs on which the many people his life had touched sat.

Alphie's death left me in a loneliness that was a kind of death in itself. For life exists only in the connections we have with those we love, and all my brothers, those who along with me had survived the horrible shackles of poverty and gone on to forge lives that mattered and would be remembered, were gone.

I was in that fog of grief as I spoke at Alphie's memorial. I barely remember what I said, nor can I recall the words of the others who spoke with passion about youngest brother: Lynn and Ellen, Frank's widow, Alphie's friends and nieces, and my son Conor.

But, of course, I gathered my wits enough to lead the congregation in song.

Maybe it was then that clarity began to displace the confusion. There in front of me were several hundred people singing, smiling, and remembering the goodness in brother Alphie.

Those faces included not only every person in my brother's life who had mattered to him but everyone who mattered in mine. And their voices carried the remembrance of all those who mattered and are now gone. Yes, Frank was there, as was Angela, and Michael, and even the old man. Yes, even he was there too.

All of them singing the sweet soft strains of "Will Ye Go, Lassie, Go":

Oh, the summertime is coming
And the trees are sweetly blooming

And the wild mountain thyme
Grows around the blooming heather
Will ye go, lassie, go?
And we'll all go together
To pluck wild mountain thyme
All around the blooming heather
Will ye go, lassie, go?

I began this tale by telling you that I don't believe in God and that my god exists in the faces of my children and grand-children and beautiful wife.

My only hope is that when I do take my last breath, my god surrounds me. If those faces are my last flickering image in life, then it really doesn't matter what comes next.

# THIRTEEN

# Departure Lounge Too

*If intercourse gives you thrombosis,*
*And continence causes neurosis,*
*I'd rather expire*
*Fulfilling desire*
*Than live in a state of psychosis.*

There's an old Irish joke about the funeral of the most hated man in Cork. In life he was a terrible person, a moneylender and a landlord who evicted the elderly, crippled, and slow-witted. He owned all the businesses in town, where he overcharged for goods, paid rotten wages, and left all his money to the church.

At the funeral Mass, the priest waxed eloquent about the dead, then asked for some words from the congregation. Nobody volunteers, so he tells Malachy to come up and say something. Malachy fumbles for a few moments, then blurts out:

"His brother was worse."

Most days now I scan the obituaries, or the Irish sports pages as they are known, and note a large number of men exactly my age who have just died, most of whom I didn't know ever lived. As the brother Alphie once said, "What a shame; people are dying these days that never died before."

Those who aren't dead yet are the walking wounded, the death marchers of my generation. You can see them every day on the streets of the Upper West Side of Manhattan, where I live. They come out with their canes, walkers, and wheelchairs after the morning rush hour, and are back in handicapped-accessible buildings well before the end of the workday. The middle of the morning is an especially abundant time for elder watching, as you'll find them on line at a Duane Reade drugstore, or flashing seniors' cards at a late-morning matinee.

Like old elephants at a watering hole in the Serengeti, the wrinkled pensioners gather at four in the afternoon at local diners for the early bird specials, meals that come complete with a small dish of rice pudding or Jell-O for dessert.

I was never a fan of Jell-O unless accompanied by custard.

I am now well into my eighties, with a medical history that has to do with supplanting the medical establishment. There may be physical limitations to my daily doings, but any day I'm on this side of the grass is a good one. Still, my list of maladies is now approaching the length of Molly Bloom's soliloquy in Joyce's *Ulysses*.

Since you asked.

I'm a cancer survivor, cured by radioactive seeds that were injected into the prostate. I had to piss them out through a tea strainer for a few weeks. By the way, you don't "battle" cancer, as the stupid overused phrase goes. You either get cured or you die from it; there is no battle.

I have nine stents implanted into my widow-maker artery to facilitate the flow of blood. I have as many stents as cats have lives.

I had a brain tumor on the auditory nerve that caused a loss of hearing in my right ear. We shrank it with radiation, but a partial deafness remains.

But for an old guy, and I say this with the utmost sincerity, nothing is more emotionally fraught than the loss of mobility. We are the unwalking dead.

My slow descent into debilitation began when I was doing a play a few years back in Vermont, and someone had the good sense to send me a card that read "Break a leg," which I did. I rehabilitated at Helen Hayes Hospital overlooking the Hudson River. Fantastic place, with wonderful people.

Not too long after, I had a knee replacement, which makes medieval torture seem like a Pilates class. But the worst was yet to come.

Diana and I were renting a house in Rhinebeck, New York. Nestled in the beautiful Hudson Valley, Rhinebeck is a jewel, filled with culture, hiking trails, and spirituality. We've been going there for years. Late one night, in the rented house, I was watching a show about Goebbels the Nazi on television when I went to the kitchen to get a snack of matzos, butter, and jelly. Marvelous combination, all crackly and sweet. I wasn't at all familiar with this particular house, and there was a step down into the kitchen, and it was dark. It felt as though I stepped off the face of the earth. When I finally hit the floor, I could hear the crack. I couldn't move. Diana was upstairs, and I didn't want to awaken her because I knew she would be disturbed all night what with the ambulances and all that. So there I was, the body stretched on the cool floor, with an overwhelming pain and nothing I could do about it. Diana and I have been meditating for years, and I tried to take my mind away from the pain by concentrating my thoughts. It was then that it came to me. Goebbels! He was wreaking vengeance on me for eating a Jewish snack, matzos!

Finally I was able to crawl my way to a first-floor bedroom and pull myself up on the bed, where I stayed until the morning. Diana was furious at me when she awoke.

"If you ever do that again," she said, "I'll divorce you."

Everything was bollixed. The paramedics couldn't get the gurney out the door because the doorways were so narrow. I had broken my hip, which is the most severe of accidents for a man or woman my age. We don't give a thought to our hips for most of our lives, and then they become as precious as the brain or heart. Fucking hip. I used to be hip, and now I had a broken one.

So they took me to the local hospital, and there I stayed until they could transport me to New York–Presbyterian Hospital, where they put in four pins. The pins didn't work, so I had to have a new hip put in ten months later. From that moment on my mobility was only a hope. On it was to a succession of wheels, both motorized and on walkers with yellow tennis balls on the bottoms of the legs. I tell you, I won't watch a single game of tennis anymore, because I have such a resentment against the balls.

———————

On top of all of that, I contracted a disease called IBM. A lengthy probe of nerves and muscles and a biopsy of some of the same produced the diagnosis. Inclusion body myositis is a condition that involves itself in the process of wasting the muscles to stringy fiber. A prescription drug for the heart had most likely caused the affliction by turning my body's immune system against itself. Apparently there is no cure or remedy for IBM, and it is, as they proclaim in medical parlance, progressive. So now my disease and my politics are in alignment.

In itself, IBM is not directly fatal, but a wheelchair is your final consignment, so it's just as bad. There are fates worse than death. The first doctor I saw wanted me to get to the wheelchair facility to be fitted for one as soon as possible. He gave me a year at the outset for any ambulatory ability on my own. If one learns anything as one reaches my age, it is that a second and third opinion are a good idea. Laddies two and three thought doctor number one had been on the dire side with his prognosis. Yes, they said, IBM had encamped in my hospitable body and, yes, it would worsen. But it would do so much more slowly than doctor number one, whom I now refer to as doctor number two, predicted. As I write this, three years have passed, and I am still hobbling about with the walker, although for trips of any distance I have a motorized contraption that I zip around in like a kid on a three-wheeler.

The thing about reduced ambling, though, is that it also affects the emotions. Over the last few months, I've been batting away and warding off the black dog, as Winston Churchill called depression. Sometimes the dog manages to penetrate my defenses and take possession of my life, expertly stressing me toward despair and approaching death. The twin of depression seems to be anger, which takes over when depression takes a nap. And off I go into the righteous rant of "Why me?" and "What did I do?" and "What the fuck is happening to me?" All these phrases are dispensed by a racing mind that frames them with dazzling visuals of all the activities I took for granted: the two-mile walks with Diana on summer mornings, the strolls on Broadway on the Upper West Side, the camping in Nova Scotia, the exhilarating rugby games of my youth, going with Diana to the Kripalu Center for Yoga & Health in Stockbridge, and never having to think about the height of a chair or couch and whether I would need help to arise from it.

What kind of joy, satisfaction, ecstasy, and laughter are present when one is slumped in a wheelchair, mouth open like a mackerel's, oozing spittle, depending on others, be they related or hired, to do the daily job of assisting a mere existence? I don't know about you, but in my gut I find death more inviting than the simulation of life in a wheelchair.

I've found that the only way to get out of the darkness is to hobble through it.

A few months back, I went to something called a death café. Sounds a bit morbid, like a cross between Starbucks and a funeral home, but it was of great help. First imagined by a Swiss psychologist, the cafés began to sprout in England. The idea is pretty simple. If you get people together and let them talk about death, it lightens the burden and fear. As it was the Brits who popularized the cafés, tea and sweet cakes are served.

There are now hundreds of these civilized discussion groups around the world, including a few here in New York City. Though there is a guide, usually some sort of professional, no psychoanalysis is offered. Rather the guide acts as a traffic cop, directing the comments and conversation. In my case, Dr. Barbara Simpson hosted the thirty or so attendees at the New York Society for Ethical Culture on Central Park West.

The first thing that struck me about the gathering was the percentage of women in the group. I attended cafés about three times, and I was in a distinct minority in each. I counted only a handful of other men. The answer to why, I think, is simple. The males of our species, especially the more macho of the sect, are more afraid of death than women. Just the thought of discussing death frightens them.

Not everyone in the room was about to die. Yes, there were a few elderly and those with terminal diseases, but there were also plenty of spouses, children, and friends of loved ones who are facing death.

What surprised me the most about the meeting was that there was a lightness in the room. In a most eloquent, intimate, and honest way, people talked about death with humor and tolerance. Most seemed comfortable with the thought of death and dying. I felt right at home.

Now, don't get me wrong, it's not as if I'm looking forward to dying, though I am curious. But I don't spend my time dwelling on that certain day. I don't know if it was me or the Buddhists who came up with the idea first (it was probably the Buddhists), but if you stay present in the moment in which you exist, you won't have any fear or apprehension about death. You'll be too busy enjoying your life to worry about something that hasn't happened yet.

As I get closer to my last, more than ever, I live my life one day at a time. I begin each of those days by telling my dear Diana that I love her. My children and grandchildren delight me. Each day I try to let go of resentments. A wise person once told me, "Let go or get dragged."

As I said, I don't drink alcohol anymore. It doesn't agree with me, and I don't agree with anyone around me when I'm drinking. One day at a time, I avoid fried foods and eat things that are good for me. Diana knows nutrition, and son Cormac is a great guide. I waste nothing. Not time, not opportunity. And certainly not food.

Each day I try to do something kind for someone else. And I believe in what Oscar Wilde said: "Always forgive your enemies; it annoys them."

On good days I make up my mind to live my life to its utmost and will continue to do so as long as the brain is still transmitting the necessary information to the functioning areas. So far so good. I urinate, excrete, eat, drink, make love (oh yes, still functioning in that department), I see, I hear, I laugh, I speak, I taste, I hug, I awaken each day, and if there is no coffin lid within three inches of my nose, I turn to tell Diana, "I love you," which are always my first words.

I eat breakfast, oatmeal one of my favorites. I use McCann's and soak the oats overnight to make them easier to digest and to release the phytic acid. This way the bod has a better chance to absorb the many nutrients the oat possesses. I'm prediabetic, so I don't use any sugar, but the fruit is a big thing in my house. I use blueberries, papaya, pears, and the one that got Adam booted out of the Garden, the apple.

After breakfast I might take a ride on the old scooter. Sometimes I'll hang a right out of my apartment building and head to Riverside Park. That's where I've told Diana to spread my ashes. There's a beautiful view of the Hudson River all the way north to the George Washington Bridge.

Years ago, when Frank was alive, our friend Brian Brown approached us with an idea. He wanted us to buy a sailboat and said he would get some of the others in our crowd to chip in. That group included Isaiah Sheffer, Gene Secunda, who was a professor of media studies at NYU, Frank, and the author Melissa Bank, among others. Brian had owned a sailboat a few years before and thought it would be a good communal activity for us. We all said yes. But the purchase of said boat kept getting delayed. One of the reasons for the delay was the difficulty of obtaining a mooring. To have a boat you need one, and a mooring in the waters off Manhattan at the time was not easy to come by. Brian put his name on a list, and it was ten years before one opened up. When it did, there was a great flurry of activity. Brian strongly suggested we move quickly on securing the mooring even though we didn't have a boat, because if the vessel ever did materialize, he said, we'd need something to hook it on to. I think the mooring cost us $1,100 each year.

So there we were, the proud boatless owners of a mooring located somewhere in the middle of the Hudson River.

The Mooring Mates met for lunch at Mike O'Neal's Boat Basin Café at Seventy-Ninth Street and the Hudson. When asked to point out the mooring in the expanse of choppy gray water, Brian waved in the general direction of the George Washington Bridge and said, "It's up there." There were at least fifty moorings for us to choose from, so we never knew which (if any) was ours. I christened it the Thomas Mystical Mooring, and the name stuck. We made a pact to meet regularly at O'Neal's for general oceanic discussion and specific talks about whether or not our mooring existed. We all took seafaring names. I was Anchors. Frank was Starbuck at first, but then thought the name "too Melvilleish" and started calling himself Hornblower. Brian was Barnacles. Melissa was Bubbles. Isaiah took the name Fletcher Jew, the Hebrew version of the name of the first mate on the *Bounty*. New members came aboard but had to pass a stringent nautical test, which included knowing the words to the song "On the Good Ship Lollipop," which became the name Gene Secunda adopted. One day Mike O'Neal offered us a canoe so we could paddle out to the middle of the river for a closer inspection. Luckily, we had the good sense to decline, or else we might have been lost at sea.

We never did buy a boat, and the exact location of the

Thomas Mystical Mooring, if it ever existed, has never been charted. But I still look for it when I go to Riverside Park.

———————

From my spot in Riverside Park, I also watch with envy as the runners and bicyclists zip by. Young mothers gather with prams at hand. I have to watch out for the wild turkeys that are now in the park. The neighborhood folk have taken to calling them Giulianis after our intrepid ex-mayor. Personally I think it's an insult to the birds. Once in a while, I'll be there to watch the sunset; its glimmering redness sets the water ablaze.

Meanwhile, I try to keep my sunset at bay.

I've been attending writing salons run by the Irish American Writers & Artists, an association of which I am a founding member, for the last five years or so. Writers of all stripes populate our salon: young, old, new, and experienced. There are novelists and short story writers, poets and songwriters. I delight in hearing the endearing written words, the marvelous stitching of them, some so beautifully bad and others sad and poignant. Some are the product of labor, a mining of each word, each one dug out painfully as if it contained gleaming gold or sparkling diamonds. Other writers just flick them on the page, where they leap about like highly trained ballet dancers, each one a figure of grace and beauty flying swiftly through the air. There are bits of novels, lively songs, and bawdy stories.

I'm having the time of my life as I sit in wonder as the

magic of lyrical elation uplifts me with boundless creativity. I feel sorry for the people who do not feast at this banquet of textured words.

Writing is a function practiced only by human beings. And at last glance I was a human. Fish, rats, turtles, donkeys, snakes, and elephants never go to literary classes or conventions, or form book clubs. Gods never write. Neither do angels. I have been seeking an autographed first edition of the Bible without success for years. No such thing exists. But with writing all things are possible. So if you want to write, write. I would love to be compensated for all the times I have heard, "Someday I am going to sit down and write a book." A lot of those folks are now lying down in a grave, and for some reason they are not writing despite being in a quiet, isolated place with no distractions. Computer availability might be a problem.

And you don't have to be Irish or American either to enjoy with us. All are welcome at our salons, whether you're Hindu, Irish, British, Mexican, or Chinese. There are no walls, just the wonder of words in an atmosphere of mutual admiration and support.

At home I write just about every day, even if it's just one of my famous lists that tickle me to no end. You know how it's *a pride of lions* and *a flock of geese*? Well, here's a list along those lines:

A backlog of bureaucrats
A lunacy of liberals
A dismal of Democrats

A constipation of conservatives
A regurgitation of religionists
A shithouse of segregationists
A gangbang of NRAers
An evaporation of evangelists
A peevish of Protestants
An anonymous of nuns
A pedophile of priests
And so on.

I write longhand with a fountain pen, as I've never been any good at typing. Longhand runs in the family. Frank wrote *Angela's Ashes* that way, although he did type it before he sent the manuscript to the editor.

I've become addicted to this Facebook thing and, you might be surprised to learn, do some ranting on it now and then. Studies say it helps you live longer (the Facebook, not the rants). Still, the responses to my diatribes amuse me to no end. I also still get a chance to talk a bit on the radio, on a show that is aired on WBAI (99.5 FM) here in New York every Wednesday. Keeps me busy and helps remove the depression.

I still go out on auditions sometimes for absurd television and radio commercials and little bits on TV shows and movies. I'm rejected more times than not, but at least I try. Recently I had an opportunity to audition for the understudy of a role in a play written by the marvelously talented, intelligent playwright John Patrick Shanley, and directed by the great director Doug Hughes. I could have done the part sitting down, which shouldn't be confused with standing on my head.

Down I went to the Roundabout Theatre Company after studying the selected audition piece and was greeted warmly by the Doug Hughes himself. I sat in the designated chair and gave a good reading, as I had memorized the piece and had made the appropriate emotional choices, as they say. Hughes thanked me, but I had to ask him to lend me a hand in getting out of the steel chair, which he did.

I have no way of knowing this for sure, but I think my handicap convinced the director that I was too incapacitated for the role. Then, a day or so later, I received a telephone call from a woman connected with the play, who said that Doug Hughes thought I gave a brilliant reading, but I was too old to have a close relationship with a forty-three-year-old son, which the role involved. I found the reasoning odd, since I have a forty-five-year-old son, Cormac, with whom I have a very close relationship. But, she said, because the recital I gave was so good, would I consider recording it for Mr. Hughes so that the people doing the role could hear how a real Irishman would speak the lines? My first reaction, you might have guessed, was to politely tell her to tell Mr. Hughes to go fuck himself. Luckily those words stayed inside the cranium and didn't escape through the mouth. Instead I spoke in a polite tone and asked if I could think about it.

Of course, she said, "Of course."

When I hung up, I made a swift call to the agent, Naomi Kolstein, to discuss if there was anything to salvage out of the wreckage. We agreed to ask for a reasonable fee, some tickets to the performance, and a program mention. I also wanted to do the recording at my apartment. Naomi rang the folks at the Roundabout, and they agreed to the terms.

The victory was small, but small victories are sometimes enough to pull you out of the depression. Even the fact that the Roundabout called back the next day and rescinded the offer didn't diminish the rise in my mood. I know a thing or two about building self-esteem, because I started with none. Poverty doesn't allow it. Now, as I wheel my way into the last chapter of this tale of mine, I do things that make me feel better about myself, like spending time with Diana, my children, and my grandchildren. As long as I remember what's worthwhile, then my life is worth living.

Diana and I will go out for dinner now and then, but mostly we eat at home. My son Cormac lives with us—as does Conor at times—and he's a great cook and a vegetarian. But both Diana and I can handle ourselves around a stove too.

I have the best recipe for mashed potatoes in the entire world. I use finely chopped onions, finely chopped garlic, olive oil, and yogurt. But the real secret is two tablespoons of horseradish. A little salt. A little pepper. And Bob's your uncle. Delightful!

Evenings are usually quiet. I'll watch some television. For a while *Downton Abbey* had my interest, I guess because it showed how the other one percent lived. I was faithful to Jon Stewart when he was on, and I continue to watch John Oliver on Sunday nights and Samantha Bee on Wednesdays.

But most of the time, I'll go into the living room, sit in my favorite chair, and read.

Diana and I moved into this apartment on West End Avenue fifty-two years ago. Three bedrooms, two and a half baths, as they say; the rent then was $215 a month. We hired your man Jack Kilcullen, who did some repairs for me at Himself, and he built the bookshelves that now surround me with authors who have enlightened my life. My collection of P. G. Wodehouse is on those shelves, as are Tolstoy and Dostoyevsky. There's a complete set of Shaw, and plenty of James Joyce, of course. Each June sixteenth, Bloomsday, many talented actors and self read excerpts of the text of the greatest novel ever written, at the Symphony Space here on the Upper West Side. For thirty years the great Isaiah Sheffer directed the night. We start the reading of *Ulysses* at seven in the evening of the sixteenth of June, and finish sometime around two the following morning with Fionnula Flanagan reading Molly Bloom. Come. Bring your tattered copy of Joyce's classic from the lit class you took in college, and read along with us. Bloomsday is truly one of my favorite days of the year.

I also have books by friends and brothers, and a bunch that I collected during my radio career. On the shelves are also other reminders of my life. There's a large photo of the doorway to the house on Schoolhouse Lane where we lived, and one of Leamy's School, and one of Angela. The letter from the father and Angela's diary are on the shelves. The ever-alert mind flashes back to the dark forbidding slum with the single lonely light of one sputtering candle, the walls gleaming with droplets of water slowly traversing the surface before reaching the bottom, collecting in little pools, and freezing overnight. And the family wrapped in old, old, worn clothes and huddled around a fire of muddied soaking-wet peat from craw-thumping merchants who marched into the church in pious rectitude after having robbed the poor.

But now it's comfortable and toasty in my living room. There are maps that Diana collected during our hiking days on the shelves. There's a photo of me in my air force uniform, the toy train that my friend Chuck Walley and Lionel gave me. There are plenty of pictures of the brothers and myself, and in every one of them we're laughing. There's a photo of my son Conor in his NYPD gear, standing in front of the just-fallen towers of the World Trade Center. There is a royalty payment check for a movie with Liam Neeson in which I made a brief appearance. The film was aptly named, for this book at least, *After.Life*. The check is for exactly one cent. Oh well, you can't take it with you. There's a small cardboard box of rubber stamps, including the one that reads, "Deceased." There's my honorary diploma from the primary school and an album I made. It contains the song "I Hate Pigeons."

I hate pigeons, they're a dirty bird
They're never clean, they are so obscene
When you're walking, it is wise to know,
Whether they are flying high or low.

We sold about three copies.

———————

There are times when, sitting in the living room, surrounded by the books, knowing there are food and beverages in the kitchen just a few steps away, I do a little self-pinching. For illumination all I have to do is flick a little lever at my elbow. There are a television, a radio, and a computer, which is still a great mystery to me, within my range of vision. Always in the vicinity is my pal, my beloved friend, the highly intelligent and never reticent Diana. Several of the sons and their children can arrive at any moment, bringing chatter, noises, chaos, and an abundance of life into the room. All the while, there I sit like some monarch, having so much joy in my life that I find it difficult to refrain from hugging myself.

The window in the room faces southwest, and during afternoon and evening in the summer it gets plenty of sunlight. Some days I'll sit in the chair and let the rays of the sun warm me. If I close my eyes, I can return to People's Park in Limerick. I'm there with Frank and Mike and Alphie, and we're kicking around a soccer ball, a real one, and afterward we walk with our arms draped over each other's shoulders and sing "Barefoot Days."

I can remember how proud I used t' be
When Dad an' Mother would buy new shoes for me
Now, that's the feeling we've all had
How new shoes would make you glad
But the best time, if you recall
When you wore no shoes at all

Barefoot days, when we were just a kid
Barefoot days, oh boy, the things we did
We'd go down to the shady brook
With a bent pin for a hook
We'd fish all day an' fish till night
But th' darn ol' fish refused to bite
How we'd slide down some ol' cellar door
We'd slide an' slide, till our pants got tore
You know, that slidin' down the cellar door
Makes your clothes tear, an' you'll get a lotta splinters
But you mustn't tell where
Oh boy, what joy we had in barefoot days

Bittersweet as it can be, sometimes the memory is a grand thing, especially when I remember that I'm still alive.

# FOURTEEN

# A Long Nap

*I do not fear Death. I had been dead for billions and billions of years before I was born, and had not suffered the slightest inconvenience from it.*

MARK TWAIN

I have tried to imagine what manner of exit I will get to experience as I expel a breath and endeavor to get it back to inflate my lungs, but alas, that last breath will have departed for places unknown.

I have no intention right now of committing suicide, although as I become more dependent and powerless, the thought of getting help in ending my life begins to whisper to me. But in some places suicide is against the law, say the naysayers. You can come and prosecute me after I do it, says I.

There are several states that allow it, and as of this writing physician-assisted suicide is on the ballot in several more. I believe they call it a "death with dignity" bill. I like that. A version of the bill is just about to become legal in the District of Columbia. I know of a few people in DC I'd like to see test the law out once it's in force. There are some doctors still against assisted suicide. They say it flies in the face of the core doctoring tenet: "First do no harm." I wonder how much harm the dying must endure for the doctors' principles.

I don't know if I have enough time to wait for a death with dignity bill to become legal in New York, and suicide by one's own hand can be a dicey proposition. I don't know enough about chemicals to ingest a fatal dose, and that kind of ignorance can leave you catatonic or totally immobile, which I would never do to Diana and my children.

I can't drive anymore, so I'm not able to speed up into a highway abutment or overpass, which reminds me of the story about the English lord who wanted to end it all. "Jeeves," he said to his chauffeur, "we're going to commit suicide. Drive off the next cliff."

I thought about taking an NRA gun safety class. There has to be a good chance that you'll get shot in one of those. Which brings to mind the other one, about the guy who catches his wife in bed with another man, goes to a drawer, pulls out a gun, and puts it to his own head.

"No, please!" the wife screams.

"Shut up," the husband says. "You're next."

I guess I could take the motorized wheelchair up Riverside Drive and to the middle of the George Washington Bridge. It must be a good place to commit suicide, every three and a half days someone tries. I know it's fine for committing political suicide. Just ask Chris Christie. Bada-boom.

But even if I could pull myself up over the railing and fall the two hundred or so feet to the Hudson, there's no guarantee that I'd end up dead. Something like 5 percent of the jumpers survive. I wonder what people must be thinking on the way down. The adage goes that your life flashes before your eyes. I don't think there would be enough time for me to see the entirety of mine.

There are hospices here in NYC run by various orgs. And they do help people to die in peace and physical comfort. I would like to end this life in one of these, if death is going to be a stretched-out affair. I have wondered about spouting the last words. I always got the impression that the last words are delivered in an oratorical fashion, deep voice, strong delivery, followed by a gasp and then a collapse into the snow-white pillow. When it comes my turn, I hope I will be free of pain, no matter the toxicity of the painkillers. And under no circumstance will there be a member of the clergy throwing water on my head or absolving my brain, hands, genitals, feet of sin by putting oil all over them.

If my family wants to witness my last exhalation then they are most welcome to hear it. Whatever got us here is also responsible for getting us outta here. Be we trees, humans, fish, stone, earth, wheat, fruit, everything is eventually reduced to one kind of dust. We humans have divided ourselves into various sects with astonishing myths about how we are created by a wizard in the sky. Some of them symbolically gobble bread and slurp wine, alleging they are the body and blood of the son of the guy they call God. Others eat other humans, believing they will ingest the bravery and intellect of their supper.

My sect has it that the God Guy picked a wife of fifteen, got her preggers with a kid named Jesus, blamed a carpenter named Joe, and got the kid to wander around babbling about his kingdom, et cetera, which got the kid executed for sedition. Not the kind of story I want to hear when I'm dying. I'll take a song, thank you. And I don't want anything to do with this heaven joint they talk to me about. It's overflowing with repentant sinners, holy people, pious pricks, reverential clergy, boring bishops, preaching pedophile priests, sermonizing saints, all of them indulging in grabbing sanctity from thin air.

What's important to me is that I will be taking leave of this body that has housed my mind and what is called spirit for almost nine decades. It's a living thing that has carried me many places on this earth. It ran me up and down many a rugby field, it was tackled and flung to the earth at frequent intervals and repaid the compliment with great satisfaction. Its fists were raised in anger when I drank too much whiskey, sometimes hitting people innocent of any offense. It has embraced the bodies of women in lust and has been faithful to one for a long time. It has been cut open by surgeons and had metal inserted to replace bones. It has shed blood, expelled body fluids, and cried tears. It has kissed and hugged my children and grandchildren. Its tongue has babbled curses, shouted inanities, and whispered loving words. Its hands have written many words.

Now it is weakened and at times immobilized, but it is still the vehicle of my mind and my thoughts, and it still smiles at the sight of my beloved Diana, and my grown and growing children.

---

As far as the old bod goes, maybe I'll just have them do as the Buddhists do, just put me out and let me decompose and let the birds eat me. Of course, we'd have to find a place where they wouldn't ticket us for littering, and I've had so much medication the birds would probably turn up their beaks at me.

I suppose I'll let them cremate me when I go, and not before. Might as well make an ash out of myself one last time. I've already made arrangements. All Diana has to do is call the company. They come pick the bod up at home or in the hospital, or wherever I die, and then transport it to New Jersey, where the crematorium is. And after I've been reduced to ashes, they'll pack me in a tidy can or plastic bag and deliver me to Diana like Chinese food. No fuss, no muss, as they once said. The whole tab is $906. I've paid it in full.

Though the Catholic Church wants you to bury ashes and not scatter them, they can kiss my ashy arse. What's the fun in cremation if you don't get to be sprinkled about on your favorite places? Not too long ago, here in New York, they stopped a performance of an opera because a man dumped his friend's ashes in the orchestra pit. They thought it was a terrorist attack.

Diana's parents were both cremated. Most of her father's ashes are behind their house in Pennsylvania. But some found their way into the Pacific Ocean. Diana and I were on a cruise from Japan to Hawaii. My wife had put a portion of her father's ashes in a sunglasses case and forgotten all about them. When she pulled out the glasses, the ashes blew over the railing and into the sea. We were passing, somewhat appropriately, Wake Island.

Diana put her mother's ashes on a raft and sent them down the Delaware River, which, near Philadelphia, finds its way into Delaware Bay and out past Cape May to the Atlantic.

If Diana's mother's ashes rode the Gulf Stream to the North Atlantic drift and then found their way into the current that flows south past the Canary Islands and, driven by the trade winds, back across the equator; and if her father's ashes took the ocean stream in the South Pacific and hopped a ride with the Antarctic Circumpolar Current, and then came north on the Benguela Current, there's a chance they met somewhere in the Caribbean.

We like to think that was the case.

Some of Frank's ashes were buried in a cemetery near where he lived in Roxbury, Connecticut. The rest of them are in the Frank McCourt Museum in Limerick. There's also a bust of him in front of the museum, formerly the Leamy Academy of Surgeons. My brother would have gotten a big kick out of that.

Portions of Mike's and Alphie's ashes are also in Limerick. My son Conor took them there and spread them in the Lanes, on Barrack Hill—some of Alphie's in front of the pub that he raced into in his pram—and also in Mungret Cemetery. There he sprinkled them on my uncle Ab Sheehan's grave marker. The rest of the ashes were put in with Frank's in the Frank McCourt Museum.

As mentioned, most of Angela's ashes are in the Mungret Cemetery too, but, as you know, some of them are on Margaret Mary's grave in Queens.

Maybe Conor will take some of mine to Limerick too, sprinkle some of them on the bank of the Shannon where I had my first spiritual journey.

Still, sometimes I think they won't have to cremate me. Instead I'll die right under a tree, and I'll be so old I'll just fall like dust and the breeze will take me across the Brooklyn Bridge again to the apartment on Clausen Avenue, and then I'll fly across the Atlantic and to Limerick, where I'll buzz right under the noses of all those who turned them up on my family and me. And I'll drop some of the dust on Mungret Cemetery and Angela's grave, but most of me will ride the winds across the sea again to be with my fair Diana. I'll just follow her like a silk scarf flowing in the breeze.

––––––––––

Death is a civil right that is granted every human being. No matter who you are, each day brings you closer to death. Of course, people call it the end not knowing what goes on after the body indulges in spiritual flatulence and boots the mind and what they say is a soul. I have to say that I'm not afraid of death. Perhaps at the precise advent and with the thoughts of what's next running wild within the cranium, some fear will invade, but most likely I'll just slip away with the comforting thought that I did the best I could.

There is some scientific evidence that consciousness may continue after death. Some 40 percent of people who survived near-death heart attacks told researchers about being aware of separating from their bodies and having a peaceful feeling of time slowing down.

I don't anticipate that as I depart the corpse I will suddenly be bounding about the terrain like a goosed gazelle, yelping, "Free at last, free at last." I don't believe in hell, so I don't think I'm headed south, and I have no desire to go to the heaven described by the faith of my youth, a place no doubt filled with pious hypocrites, born-again arseholes, and conservatives. Thank God I'm an atheist.

Rather, I think my death will be sleep that knows no waking, followed by a wake that knows no sleeping. I'll have an RIP, requiescat in pace, more generally known as rest in peace, as if there is another way to rest. I know I'm not going to be laid to rest, because I know of no human who can rest while getting laid.

If consciousness does continue after death, I'd like to witness my funeral. Like Tom Sawyer, I'll hide up in the rafters and listen to all the lovely things said and all the humorous anecdotes. There's plenty of material from which to choose. I went from being a slum kid to visiting the White House, from failed beach Bible salesman to best-selling author. I've had encounters with the famous, infamous, and funny. In 2008 I ran on the Green Party ticket for the office of the governor of the State of New York. I received forty-eight thousand votes and said I would demand a recount if I won.

From the rafters I'd also inflict chronic diarrhea on anyone I see who uses that dopey and vacant phrase "Our thoughts and prayers are with you."

But I don't think I'd like to see Diana crying. Nor would

I like to see the sad expressions on the faces of my children, Malachy, Siobhan, Conor, Cormac, and Nina, or tears in the eyes of my grandchildren, Mark, Gillian, Adrianna, Reilly, Cassidy, Gus, Fiona, and Cole. I'd want to come down from said rafters and comfort them. Sit next to my lovely wife one more time and let her lay her head on my shoulder.

Once, during a driving rainstorm in Ireland, I picked up an old man on the road. When he got out, he said to me, "Thank you, sir, for your kindness. May you have a happy death."

I thought it was an odd wish until I started thinking about his words. If I have a happy death it means I've lived a happy life, or, rather, that I've learned how to live a happy life.

If you could substitute the word *love* for God or Jesus or Muhammad or Moses or any other deity or prophet, I would be the most religious person in the world. I don't know if your love dies with you or not, but I don't think it does. The living keep it alive, and even after I go it will remain in microscopic particles that float in the air for all time, I hope.

So breathe deeply, children, and have faith in the kingdom of goodness within you. My advice to you is to live each day as if it's your last, and one day you'll be right.

There are those who say that the hearing is the last of the senses to shut down when you die. So if you happen to be there when I go, make sure you sing me a song. "Will Ye Go, Lassie, Go?" is the one that would send me off with a smile.

All together now, children:

Oh, the summertime is coming
And the trees are sweetly blooming

And the wild mountain thyme
Grows around the blooming heather
Will ye go, lassie, go?
And we'll all go together
To pluck wild mountain thyme
All around the blooming heather
Will ye go, lassie, go?
I will build my love a tower
Near yon pure crystal fountain
And on it I will pile
All the flowers of the mountain
Will ye go, lassie, go?
And we'll all go together
To pluck wild mountain thyme
All around the blooming heather
Will ye go, lassie, go?

And just remember, when you stop getting older you're
dead.

# Acknowledgments

My profound thanks to Kate Hartson, who cast a warm eye on this death book. And my thanks to my perceptive agent, Laurie Liss, for her counsel and skillful care of the difficult details. To my beloved Diana, spouse/wife/friend/inspiration, for the half century of delicious hugging love. And to my collaborator and friend Brian McDonald, a man of great humor and patience. A man of the Word and of his word. Gratitude will have to do.